The Spiritual Exercises of St. Ignatius

BY JAMES R. DOLAN, SJ

ISBN# 0-9632750-5-4

Imprimi Potest
Rev. Kenneth Gavin, SJ
New York Provincial
January 18, 2001

Censor librorum
Rev. Thomas E. Clarke, SJ
January 3, 2001

ISBN# 0-9632750-5-4

Foreword

My intention in rewriting was first, to make the paragraphs come alive, making each one as far as possible understandable and applicable for the first time retreatant. Second, I wanted to give the annotations distinguishing labels as an easy reference and for the purpose of an equitable dialogue. Third, I collated some Scripture texts appropriate for the initial stages of the retreat and finally I used the "presupposition" not just as it was intended, for the retreatant and director to find the positive intention in each other's dialogue but I applied it to each instruction and exercise within the text itself that it might be seen in the most positive light.

While using Fr. Puhl's version of the Spiritual Exercises for many years and later Fr. Fleming's modern version, I still needed to explain, translate and challenge the written texts. I did it so often that I developed marginal notes that became sufficient for either a series of articles or another contemporary text. I chose the latter.

One practical benefit concerns the Annotation numbers themselves. Ignatius himself labeled many of his paragraphs with terms such as "First Prelude, First Point, First Rule, Note I, Additional Direction." Wherever possible I applied a title to each of the other paragraphs that attempts to give some indication of the content.

The second benefit was to make every paragraph understandable, using laymen's language and using contemporary theological concepts, whether it concerned creation as an irrefutable and original blessing or incarnation and redemption as a validation of our intimate connection with Christ and our eternal oneness with God.

I would like to give thanks to the many retreatants that journeyed with me through the years using these Exercises. During regularly scheduled directed retreats, the Jesuit and guest staff would exchange ideas that exposed our own biases and religious conditioning. We helped each other find the spirit of the Exercises and apply the original charism and vision to benefit the retreatants.

In Particular my gratitude is extended to Thomas Clarke, SJ, David Fleming, SJ and Peter Schineller, SJ who did timely, detailed and critical evaluations of the manuscript. Cathy O'Neil was ready once again to provide the liturgical and Celtic artwork.

Unceasing respect and gratefulness goes to Tony deMello, SJ

who lived and loved the Exercises, and through his gifted style in therapy sessions, lectures, stories and guided meditations made the Christian message of freedom and love come alive for people on every continent. Tony was an inspiration for me while I was with him in Syracuse, New York for many summers and he was especially stimulating in India during my tertianship year.

My hope is that retreat directors and retreatants will delight in their spiritual journey with these Exercises as a help. They still have the responsibility to make this Ignatian Message come alive by becoming contemplatives in action and by their faith manifested in good works. Claiming the presence of God within and sensing the presence of God in so many others is visibly witnessed by a joyful life, transparent compassion and works of justice.

PREFACE

The "Spiritual Exercises" were experienced by Ignatius of Loyola and written down at the request of his fellow Jesuits for the benefit of future retreatants. It was with much urging from his companions and only after much prayer that Ignatius recorded some of his personal insights.

Iñigo, as his friends called him, was born into an aristocratic Basque family in 1492. He was a proud soldier until the age of 29 when he suffered a severe leg wound in the battle of Pamplona. When he was captured by the French they helped him to a hospital. What a shocking realization it must have been to be spared and helped by his enemy! What a change of heart must have occurred when he reflected on this profound gesture!

While this injury terminated one career, it launched him in a new direction, on a somewhat delayed vocation which touched the world of his day and is still effecting ours.

During his slow and painful recovery, he had much time to meditate on his past life. He had seen the greed and the honors that had driven his peers; he had witnessed the results, the suffering, fear and violence. While restricted by his crippled state, he asked for books on chivalry. Instead they brought him holy books on the life of Christ and one on the lives of the saints. To his surprise these readings lifted his spirit and left him with a special sense of consolation that lasted long after he had closed the books. So he searched out these inspired stories to see what in particular brought him to this exceptional peace of mind and heart. He hoped to discover a direction for peace in his turbulent world, a peace that had eluded even the mightiest rulers of his time.

Can you envision Iñigo on retreat, waking up from his illusions and the goals that had guided his life prior to his injury at Pamplona? How important it had been for him to receive praise from royalty and approval from military officers! He had been in the nobility vying for power and he had succeeded. At one time he would have done almost anything for honor and glory and the praise of his superiors.

Ignatius underwent several operations on his leg and was immobilized for a year. While recovering, he re-examined his definition of success, reflected on whether he had ever really served God's people, and whether he had truly done anything for Christ. Had he used his time and energy to further the kingdom, to bring peace to God's people, or had he spent his life testing who was more powerful, who could conquer more territory or collect more honors? After in depth and serious reflection, he confessed the sins of his past life, gave his fine clothes to a beggar and surrendered his sword to the statue of Mary at the monastery church in Monserrat. From this deliberate ritual of surrender Ignatius began a whole new life full of drama, wonder and grace.

IGNATIUS' OWN RETREAT. Ignatius began a lengthy retreat at Manresa in Spain searching for answers, searching for God. He was not a priest, not a religious, not even a pious layman. Little did he realize that in the likeness of Christ, he would melt swords, assuage fears and inspire hearts in the succeeding four centuries in every part of the world, far beyond his hometown of Azpeitia.

Twenty years after the initial notes were written in the cave of Manresa, Ignatius finished the edition that attempted to describe his weeks of prayer, his personal conversion and the mystical confirmation that accompanied his contemplations. His whole life had been transformed by his unconditional trust in God. He developed a boundless energy for study that attracted many followers, yet he delighted in the quiet time he spent in prayer. With all of his interest in learning and meditation, his heart was inflamed with love for the poor. He seemed to make special things happen wherever he went, whatever he did.

There were many other dramatic events in Ignatius' life that led him wholeheartedly to follow Jesus, but the retreat at Manresa was a dramatic interior journey that could be written in detail, meditation by meditation.

YOUR RETREAT. As we begin these exercises we are at a juncture in our journey as Ignatius was. We are truly adventurers. Actually, we are curious and gregarious by nature. Yet, we will not experience enlightenment until we understand the illusions and the conditioning that govern our lives. Let us trust that God in His goodness will show us the way as He did Ignatius, that

God will open our hearts to recognize the love that fills our lives, so that we can fully respond.

We start these exercises with the assurance that God will give light to our minds, and perception to our conditioning, so that we will understand our prejudices. Then, with greater clarity we will experience life, for we will be aware of the biases through which we have viewed it.

During these exercises we trust that God will give us the grace to see clearly and the courage to respond fearlessly and candidly. We ask God to grant us life, energy, and enthusiasm one day at a time. We pray that we can desire great things without ambition, spiritual greed, or the craving that leads to disappointment. We hope for satisfying results by giving our word, our life and our energy to this graced task. Then we will respond to God's call with understanding and transparency.

We approach these exercises trusting that God will work great wonders in us as God lowers our expectations to meet His created reality, and raises our ideals to approach His uncreated presence. When we leave our compulsive world of fears and righteousness, we discover a delightful challenge in God's creation and we can truly find God in all things. It is to this that we are called. In union with God we find our joy and happiness. Like the disciples at Emmaus, we feel our hearts stirring, our vision clearsighted, our whole being dancing.

TABLE OF CONTENTS

INTRODUCTORY OBSERVATIONS

FIRST WEEK

FOUR ADDITIONAL DIRECTIONS

GENERAL EXAMINATION OF CONSCIENCE

PENANCE

THE KINGDOM OF CHRIST

SECOND WEEK
FIRST DAY

SECOND DAY

THIRD DAY

FOURTH DAY

FIFTH DAY

THIRD WEEK
FIRST DAY

SECOND DAY

THIRD TO SEVENTH DAY
**ADDITIONAL MYSTERIES ON THE LIFE OF CHRIST
FROM JESUS BEFORE PILATE TO THE SEPULCHRE**

FOURTH WEEK
FIRST DAY

SECOND TO FIFTH DAY
**ADDITIONAL MYSTERIES ON THE
RESURRECTED LIFE FROM THE APPARITION TO
MARY MAGDALENE TO PENTECOST**

THE AD AMOREM

INTRODUCTORY OBSERVATIONS

1. PREPARATION FOR RETREAT

One of the main purposes of these Spiritual Exercises is to bring interior peace to one's heart and soul, by removing whatever tends to agitate or cause division. Often the attachments that have caused problems in relating to others or in progressing in life were initially positive. They were important and even necessary at a particular time in one's life. Therefore, it is significant as we prepare to rid ourselves of these attachments, that we treat them as former friends. Once they had value to us, we can even be grateful for how they helped us cope on certain occasions. But there is a time to say goodbye and this might be the graced moment. Ignatius says that it is important to highlight those attachments that are excessive, that are no longer useful, that are disorderly and interfering. These differ from the ones that still are constructive or necessary. Once we realize this fact, we will be gentle rather than violent with ourselves as we deal with them. There will be no fear of loss or of self-rejection. We are not our attachments.

Each of the exercises is a step to prepare us to let go of our attachments. Using them, we will be able to seek, find, and experience the will of God.

The will of God for us is a very lively, creative, expansive experience. Ignatius used to call this delight, "consolation". When you sense what you actually see, feel, smell, taste and hear, you are getting in touch with reality. Consolation is not just private and fleeting, it is an action that is enduring. It enlightens the day and the people around you; this consolation pervades your daily work and your contact with people. What lifts you up or brings you satisfaction in these sensory images? Reflect on what moves your heart.

What is important during this retreat is for you to discover the spiritual exercises that are rewarding, stimulating and realistic for you. Notice, too, that some of the exercises will work on specific days better than on others. Occasionally, you will derive consolation while doing the same thing at the same time on a regular basis. There is an ease and security that comes from orderliness. To determine if this is an attachment giving you true joy or simply a respite from the discomfort of making decisions is something that you will need to discover.

St. Ignatius uses an interesting phrase, "attachments that are inordinate." How can we describe these inordinate attachments? Let us liken them to the projections that occur when various filters are inserted on a camera. Our conditioning and upbringing are like filters layered on life. When we live and see things today with the filters of the past, distortion and illusions are created and appear as reality. When we actually become attached to the filters and their projections of life, we have a disordered attachment. How much more exciting it would be if we could discover our unconscious filters, dispose of the ones that are most distracting and see reality as it really is!

There is a certain attraction as well as an attachment that comes with illusions. When we see a magician, we enjoy being fooled or stunned. It seems true that learning the secret of the trick takes away the thrill. The fascination with illusion is universal. This condition is almost invisible and is commonly referred to by Ignatius as an "adversary." The purpose of selected readings for meditation and the assistance of an experienced director can stimulate our awareness, challenge our thinking, and make our retreat a truly 'wake-up' experience.

Illusions that have been formed over many years may have originated from our idealism, our need for approval, the influences of authority, or the promises and dreams of a better tomorrow. They have seduced goodwilled and well-meaning authorities into riding roughshod over minds and hearts and wills, usually of the young and impressionable.

St. Ignatius wanted people to be led not by the influences of others but by the gentle consolation of God's presence in each discovery, without self-rejection and without discouragement.

2. KEEP IT SIMPLE

When you meditate, or look at life from your heart's perspective, begin with the simplest of truths. Let grace uncover the mystery that pervades reality, and let yourself feel the reaction. You will notice that you are filled with truth and goodness. Despite all outward appearances, you are surrounded by a world created out of love, created in goodness, and replete with truth.

Introduction

While getting in touch with your interior feelings and your perspective on the outside world, you will experience joy and adventure in the discovery. To see things clearly enables you to appreciate; to be with people without fear provides the atmosphere for intimacy. From contemplating and experiencing these realities, you discover the mystery of human fulfillment. And the foundation of all mystery is God, the Creator.

Finding good in all things, like finding God in all things gives a wonderful sense of consolation. It enables us to see through all the inordinate attachments upon which we have depended. When we see things as they really are, our hearts are full and we cease to be greedy for more.

This is what we are called to in meditation: to have moments of vision based on reality, moments of wisdom based on truth. When you meditate you see for yourself. You are not listening to or relying on the words of another. Just as you breathe with your own breath, and see what your eyes see, the subjects that you meditate on are for your heart only - the smell of a flower, the song of a bird, the travels of an ant, the love of a friend.. How easily you can feel united with God! How comforting to know that you are the fulfillment of God's plan!

3. TYPES OF PRAYER

While practicing these Spiritual Exercises you will find many different levels of relating, but here are three.

SEEKING. The first is a trustful searching for something to happen or for someone to appear, similar to the curiosity we feel in anticipation of a private audience with a dignitary. Perhaps a gentler analogy would be the wonder as we watch and wait for the sunrise, take a walk in a new park, or climb an unfamiliar site.

AWARENESS. The second phase in these Spiritual Exercises is an interior awareness of the way our minds reason and reflect in traditional, logical ways. We become aware of the patterned fashion of our thoughts, their unusual and sporadic leaps and insights. They expose us to other levels of understanding, helping us to make connections and personal syntheses that make us feel like new creations.

COLLOQUY. A third kind of prayer exercise, expressions of the heart, is called "colloquy" or affective prayer. It is based on a deep feeling of belonging and feeling one with God.

Experiencing fellowship in a family or in a liturgical community enables us to reach out, relate and have a sense of belonging. This intimacy leads to natural and spontaneous expressions.

Prayer leads us to discover the inside treasure, and frees us to celebrate with the community, as we exchange the Good News with each other. It also has a serene phase that is very precious and leads us to a quiet depth within.

Sometimes we cannot discover our true selves until we express to others our intentions and motives; then we are able to see ourselves as mysteriously connected with one another, continuously redefining who we are in our goodness and limitations. We then will be satisfied with the one that God has made, and accept and share ourselves, with our weaknesses and strengths, our discovered side and our unexplored mystery. We can accept our vulnerability and rest in the darkness without hungering for the light; we can rest in the quiet and the private without craving for appreciation and notoriety and applause. At this stage we can enjoy the silence and the tears maybe even more than the laughter and the dancing. We can understand creation, others, and the deeper mystery of ourselves. So many things bring us to union with God. This is the beginning of the freedom we are called to, the freedom that enables us to love others. This awareness is within our reach. We can give ourselves without fear and take a chance with our talents, words and actions. These exercises are meant to be a way of freedom, a way of redemption, a very interesting way of announcing Good News.

4. OVERVIEW

This Thirty Day retreat is divided into four parts referred to as Weeks. The First Week, usually the lengthiest, is devoted to the consideration and understanding of the inordinate attachments that we live with or encounter each day. Each one of us has particular inclinations, some more powerful than others, that in varying degrees detract us from our own basic peace. The fact that they are disordered or in disarray is the key to their confusing signals and reactions. When our attachments and attractions are ordered these inclinations provide profound levels of contentment.

Inordinate attachments can be of a variety of types: praise that confuses and sometimes poisons us, apparent goods that distract us, deprivation which makes us greedy, indoctrination that paralyzes the mind, habits that cause robotic behavior, fear of rejection that upsets us, and the striving for ideals that frustrates us. These are some of the many types of inordinate attachments that are worth examining during this First Week.

For some to recognize their own biases, inclinations and attachments might require many hours of meditation and reflection. Each person must go at his or her own pace.

The intention of these meditations is to awaken people so that they might see the truth for themselves. It is as if their eyes were opened to the reality of life; and with this awareness they saw clearly, felt personally, and responded accurately. The goal of these exercises is sensitivity to life. Enjoying life will be the fruit. And so a person needs to be aware of the conditioning that has prevented him from seeing and feeling, from living as a spirit-filled creative human being.

The Second Week offers a series of exercises to help a person discover a precious value system, one that is not a duplication of the world's values or a conglomeration of past conditioning. The inspiration for rejoicing in one's own vocation will be found in meditating on the humanity and vocation of Christ from His Incarnation to His triumphal entry to Jerusalem.

In presenting a realistic following of Christ, the Third Week will treat the Last Supper, the events of Jesus' trial, the sentence imposed, then His passion, death, burial, and concluding with the reactions of His followers and other witnesses.

The Fourth Week is dedicated to the Resurrection experiences of the relatives and disciples of Jesus. The Descent of the Spirit enabled them to find the purpose of their lives and the courage to follow the call of Jesus. He who had been the favored of the Father gave His life and had risen to new life. He promised we would rise to new life too, since we were equally the favored of God. What good news for the early Christian community! What great news for the Church! What good news for you and me!

5. YOU ARE ONE WITH GOD

In beginning this process called "The Exercises" it is helpful if the retreatant feels a sense of trust and freedom as well as desire. Trust means that one has already felt accepted and chosen by God. Trust means that one feels personally invited to undertake these Exercises and feels the grace and freedom to respond with ease. It means that one is in the arms of God and that God will be divinely generous with His affection, favors and gifts. This is not a test as in a classroom where one will be given praise, criticism or a grade. It is more like coming home, to a welcoming experience, a comfortable atmosphere that is quiet and intimate. It is a transfiguration experience, yet no more dramatic than the sunset.

As a result of this sense of trust, one begins to see more clearly. Thinking then becomes more original and creative. Behavior changes in even trivial matters for one senses the accepting presence of God who is friend.

There is no obligation to wait for permission or compete for approval. So there is no obligation to be or to do anything special. One need not strive to conform to a set of standards. There is a basic ongoing incentive to follow one's heart, to listen to its inspirations and to respond to its graces. As you proceed with these exercises trust, readiness and freedom will be gifts you will perceive.

6. AWARENESS, AWARENESS, AWARENESS

St. Ignatius believes that when people are performing spiritual exercises they are getting in touch with the deepest part of themselves. Think of a child crawling toward a desired object or contemplating a little insect. Sometimes there is overflowing and uncontainable joy in the simple things of life. We can become enraptured by the wonder of it all. People who are aware have a joy that can be described as consolation. While their joy is interior, they experience nourishment from a wide variety of external encounters.

For people who are in touch with life there is also restlessness, trouble and confusion, for life is not always serene. There are challenges when an aware person is faced with a government that is insensitive to the handicapped, the underprivileged, the destitute; it is disillusioning when a person who sees clearly is confronted by a church that feels its mission is converting people and enforcing laws on its constituents. There are daily frustrations when one is faced with people who are obviously destructive but who think their behavior is justifiable. Those who are aware feel the anguish of their brothers and sisters. They realize that fear, righteousness, envy and greed lead to widespread injustice and violence against humanity.

Awareness is as powerful as a complete change of heart and as gentle as waking up. It requires an extraordinary amount of grace and patience, though the primary quality is the willingness to see. Prophets always pray for light and guidance so that they might see.

At times, celebration and euphoria can be characteristic of one who is awake and responding to life. At other times there is a businesslike attitude, a firm resolve to respond and make a difference. Consolation takes on many forms therefore, from the quiet of a mystic in contemplation, and the action of a nurse during an operation, to the experience of a peacemaker negotiating a truce.

A spirituality that is awake to present reality is really the only true spirituality. What will help us to discover whether we are living under illusions and making decisions based on past images? When you smell a flower does it give you joy? When you eat a pizza does it give delight? When you are with a friend can you feel the rhythms of life being exchanged?

You are the center, you are the one who receives and gives life; you are the responder to joys and sorrows, to consolation and desolation, to intimacy and fear. As a responder you receive, participate, and make things happen. When people live as responders during the day, they find it rather easy to sleep at night.

7. HONEST COMMUNICATION

Here Ignatius gives some instructions to the director regarding desolation. Desolation is characterized by underlying feelings of inadequacy, unworthiness, insecurity, non-acceptance or powerlessness. These feelings are the opposite of consolation. Ignatius immediately accepts these feelings as facts. For someone who does not feel accepted by God, the director's job is to accept the feeling and then inquire what exactly would make this person feel adequate and empowered. To detect the symptoms of desolation is the first step to diagnosis. By trusting the person enough to ask what he thinks would be the cure and would give some valuable clues regarding the source of the desolation.

There is extraordinary wisdom in letting a person explain why he feels inadequate. The person develops trust by having someone listen to him. Once his feeling of inadequacy is understood and appreciated, he can separate the sense of inadequacy from the actual reality of being adequate. Gentle light pierces the inner darkness when one is able to communicate honestly about one's fear of God, confusion about life, and talk about one's particular anxiety.

If we let a person describe what it is like to feel unacceptable, it may reveal what particular conditioning is at the root of such a negative attitude. At the same time, the encouragement of the director helps the person to feel valued and to realize that he is infinitely more than his thoughts about himself.

First, start with the acceptance of the person. It is the first step and it works. Watch what happens with this graced attitude. Will kindness and gentleness succeed? Does light dispel darkness? When there are many restrictions and demands made on people, they begin to believe that their goal in life is to conform and produce.

Second, the director must express an understanding of the world, its limitations, of fear in its many disguises and also the presence of disruptive people. The good that a person tries to do is often unrewarded or misunderstood. We live in a suspicious and cynical world. Unfortunately, we are often misjudged for our best efforts. When we discuss our own experiences of injustice, unfairness and inequality, we identify with the retreatant. In this acceptance and empathy, consolation can be realized. Desolation is quite a normal thing for people who endure unexpected tragedy, personal disappointments and daily disillusionment.

Third, Ignatius suggests preparing the retreatant who is going through desolation for eventual consolation. How will you dispose yourself for the advent of joy when the pain of desolation subsides? As you start thinking of the coming consolation, your thoughts and feelings naturally brighten the state that had been preoccupied with down feelings.

8. TYPICAL INCLINATIONS

There are certain times during the retreat when it will be profitable to refer to the Rules of Discernment, Annotations # 313 - 327, and # 328 - 336, to review with your director their most effective implications. These deal with the different tendencies, desires and types of inspirations that are normally encountered when one takes a spiritual journey of this length and type.

9. BE REALISTIC

Ignatius was intent on getting the retreatant and the director to be aware of the challenges imminent in the retreat process. And so the preparations for meditations and the initial directions are detailed. Often when obstacles are understood clearly they lose their bluntness, their shadow, and their ability to discourage. Some obstacles seem overwhelming, like moving a stone house, changing a twenty-year habit, or improving a relationship that has withered. To see them as difficult as well as a challenge is valuable; to see them as requiring attention and work is invaluable. Seeing good effects from the slightest modifications can be encouraging. Sometimes by simply lowering one's expectations, or by changing one's sights from the ideal product to the immediate task provides surprising success. One thing and one day at a time can make life meaningful and enjoyable.

One of the common obstacles one encounters even on retreat is "What will others think?" There is a certain embarrassment when we change our behavior patterns; there is a desire that people accept us, that they neither overreact to our presence nor dismiss us. Obtaining "permission," being considered "okay," doing what is "right" are natural tendencies although they often lead to an insecure kind of dependency where we hunger for total support before we do anything. It is helpful to be reminded of the power we allow others to have over us. It is not the physical chains that weigh us down, but the degree of mental influence by others (in our heads) that shackles us.

What will the family think when they notice a change in your behavior? People truly desire progress, improvement, and change but they do not want anything to be different. "What people think" instills greater anxiety than any actual alteration could inflict. It is such an intricate part of the fabric of our society. As we move into new horizons we are never sure if we are right; we are never sure if decisions will really work, or how long they will last. There are so many unknowns in each day that seem to make worry a legitimate option. And even when the present is tolerable we often ask, "What will the future hold?"

When persons have been raised in or supported by a repressive institution, they find themselves with an ambiguous love/hate relationship. They are acquainted with the repression they were subjected to, so they recognize it in family, ecclesial, military, and

economic structures, but are often helpless. Equality and dialogue, freedom and understanding seem foreign and any structure
whose foundation is compassion rather than dominance becomes
suspect.

It is good to know the nature of desolation and the causes of
discouragement as one understands the principles of the retreat.

10. TRUST YOURSELF

People passing through the stages of their lives gradually
detach themselves from things that are past, just as people living
in the present say goodbye to yesterday. We are always growing
in freedom from authority, past habits and ideologies that were
necessary at previous periods of our lives. This retreat provides
awareness time for stages that we are still experiencing. We trust
the new spirit within and hear the fresh call of present reality. We
are able to live in peace, in a celebrating, sharing and non-violent
way.

Sometimes the people we associate with are so influenced by
religious approval or secular accomplishments that we imitate them
and ignore our heart's desires. Temptation comes from all sides and
from the most surprising persons. The appearance of something as
right or good, because some authority says so, can be a tremendous
attraction and seems to demand our conformity. While we remember that all things that God made are good, we must not be fooled
by the goodness. We accept appearances simply as appearances,
and statements as statements. Though we accept that what others do
might be right for them, we are aware that the good is limited, that
good is relative and that goodness depends on whether this is good
for me at this time. So one's own perception and personal response
are as essential as the goodness itself.

Who would deny that rain is good? But rain for three days
destroys homes and property and neighborhoods. So it is not
good at certain times and places and in excessive quantities. And
so the ability to distinguish and the willingness to appreciate and
examine not only when something is good for me but how good
it is, is part of the ongoing discernment that occurs during these
reflective experiences and exercises.

Once again the clarity of the good can be looked at when we
discover our desires for it, our joy in it, and subsequently the
peace and consolation that results for ourselves and the commu-

nity. We will not be misled nor rejecting on the basis of appearances. We will not be deceived by the label of good or the authority that claims something is good, but rather we will be able to determine its goodness through personal experiment, dialogue and prayer.

11. STAYING IN THE PRESENT

As one goes about the process and commitment of thirty days of meditations, there is a tendency to want to reach the goal of completion, as if somehow things will be better when "this" is over with. Some people have been so conditioned in life to finish what they start that they miss the joy in the doing; they have become totally focused on the possible and expected reward - even during retreat. If this worldly attitude creeps into the retreat, be mindful that life is not something to be completed, nor to be approved of, and neither is prayer. Life occurs within this day, not after a number of days. Life occurs in the moment, in each breath and thought, not in the quantity of moments. Eternal life is now. God is found in the now. So as one finds himself looking beyond the first week of retreat, or beyond this day's prayer or even looking beyond this hour to the next one, let him be aware that even though this is a normal distraction, this is "the" hour, now is the acceptable time. God is in the present, not in the future - not in goals or in the completion of some feat.

Once again, stay with the time that God has created for you. This is the future that was created for you yesterday. A day at a time! Take what you can from this day and give what you are to this time. You will enjoy a wonder-filled retreat experience.

12. RIGIDITY AND EFFORT

If a person were working or reading he might need to stop what he is doing when it is time for another appointment. In this series of exercises there are certain time requirements. Be careful not to treat the time periods rigidly or magically. Once a time is specified by an authority or even by myself there is something "official" connected with the hour, like loyalty or fidelity. It is like doing exercises prescribed by a doctor; if he says bend and stretch your arm for fifteen minutes three times a day, and you do it only twice, is it enough? If you go over the recommended limit, do you get extra credit or are you overdoing it? And so by specifying a time like an hour, there could occur an obsession with rules that can distract from prayer and the meditation.

Another critical quality is the awareness that each person needs to determine the effectiveness of these exercises. It is important to remember that a certain thing that we do in life might take us fifteen minutes, but on another day it will take one hour or more. So we must be careful to avoid the notion that an hour is perfect, more than an hour is excellent and less than an hour is inadequate. Is a fifty minute hour sufficient? Do not let time be an obstacle or an idol.

When people made retreats in the past, they felt that many preparations, previews and preludes had to be performed assiduously. Even within the prayer time there were specific partitions of activities and dissections of time.

To keep the prayer periods simple, be aware that you are giving as well as receiving in these exercises. Be sure to take some nourishment from this investment of your time and be sensitive to the normal tendency to measure. As you read a story to a child, he delights in the simple parts of the book - a picture, a character or a familiar phrase, and he finds joy in different places each time he reads the same book. So the fruit of our prayer is the same as we would find in other life experiences. What brings us joy is not necessarily planned; sometimes we find peace where we least expect it. In finding peace, we become aware that we will not accomplish our desires by measuring God's grace, our efforts or our successes. More and more we are convinced that everything is gift.

13. PATIENCE

Ignatius reminds the retreatant that in a period of consolation you are frequently unaware of the time. Whether alone in a dark room, taking a walk, or studying a difficult text; for in consolation all things are easy. If you are going through a period of desolation all things may be unpleasant, even eating your favorite meal or spending time with your best friend. So too in prayer, some of the experiences you undergo appear to be little more than going through the motions. The same experience could be celebration if it were a time of consolation.

Basically, do not change your patterns while you are in desolation; keep your schedule and make no decisions. When you are functioning with peace and joy you will act effortlessly with even difficult tasks. You will feel extra strain and anxiety when you are not seeing clearly or you are not sure where you are going. But if you trust that God is here, and the path is still there, you might be patient with life and with yourself until the visibility improves.

14. FOLLOW YOUR HEART

The Exercises of St. Ignatius are not meant to indoctrinate anyone into a program. The spirituality of St. Ignatius is meant to be a daily awakening through exercises of awareness and sensitivity. Ignatius wanted these exercises to be ongoing, lifegiving, a true wake-up spirituality. This is epitomized by the great consolation and fervor that the retreatant feels during retreat. It can be so profound that there is a desire to dedicate one's life to a particular cause, to resolve to do something special. This might include choosing a form of direct service to others, an intimate sharing of your life, or even risking your life for the good of others.

Ignatius uses strong words of forewarning and admonishment, "Do not be inconsiderate or hasty". He advises us to be sober in examining the hindrances that could occur in carrying out these resolutions as well as the benefits or results. In examining these questions and answers, actual motives will surface. Is a person being led by imagination, devotion and hope for reward, or influenced by deprivation or indebtedness? Hopefully, a resolution will bring joy not only in the moment of fervor, but throughout one's whole life. It is not a surrender, a deprivation or a sacrificial offering but a gift, and great joy in the awareness of the gift. Also any resolution must be your choice, not that of your parents or your spiritual director, but clearly something that you want without feelings of compulsion or submission. In an honest way, you must be able to say that you are acting according to your own self-interest. This makes it a personal choice, rather than a denial of your personal choice.

Ignatius mentions that a vow or promise might be more meritorious than simply performing an action. To go to the store for yourself or because you love another is one thing. When you do not wish to go, yet go because you promised, there is a different force involved. A verbal resolution to go to the store can seem as powerful as the reality and action of actually going. Is one's word more meaningful or more effective than one's action? There is a future orientation when a person says, "I will go," but the fact is that "the going" is the reality. In one sense, the act is far greater than a person's promise and yet the promise presents a vivid and powerful statement in itself. It is a disposition of oneself for the future, a future which is really not at the person's disposal. More meritorious? Come and see. As Ignatius previously has cautioned, the retreatant filled with zeal and grace and a desire to serve should avoid making great decisions while emotionally influenced. He also warns against making important decisions for a person who is discouraged and not seeing clearly.

15. INSPIRATION AND DIRECTION

Ignatius reminds the director that the retreatant will be going through some profound reflective experiences, viewing himself and the world and analyzing his own ability to make a contribution. There is the probability that the retreatant will want to make an 'election'. While the director might encourage the retreatant to a particular way of life or to a particular promise, the main role of the director is to enable the retreatant to communicate with the Creator directly and to facilitate the devout person's quest of God's will. This is the sole disposition of the director whose directions ought to provide clarification and understanding of what is happening. By his listening presence he will assure the retreatant that he is not alone. That will diminish any fear that the retreatant might have of going to extremes.

The director's presence is significant and important, but it is equally important that the director avoids interpreting the meaning of God's graces. For the director certainly does not know God's plan for this person, or even the individual graces that this person receives each day. So if the director is aware of his own limitations he will not be persuaded to lean to one side or another, but will offer a fresh perspective, and will provide a fine balance while the retreatant is experiencing a call by God to be and to serve in the world as God's child and friend.

16. UNDERSTANDING ONE'S ATTACHMENTS

If the retreatant discovers any specific inordinate attachment to a certain thing that seems to control his life, or if he realizes that he had a strong inclination that has affected his previous decisions, he should neither reject this attachment nor reject himself. The person needs to examine his situation in the presence of God's love for him. The discovery itself is grace in action.

One may contrast one's attachments and inclinations with God's love for mankind and God's love for this retreatant in particular. Hopefully the awareness of God's love and grace will put attachments into perspective, so they will not be a burden to the person. Being able to recognize craving and possessiveness as part of one's conditioning rather than as one's fault diminishes the self-doubt and removes guilt.

So once these attachments are understood as heavy, unnecessary baggage, the grace to drop them comes immediately. Love is born, for there is nothing as clearsighted as love. The attachment admittedly provided brief security and even a kind of excitement but it does not provide the peace that only God, only love can give. Therefore, the first discovery is to see, to observe with a clear mind and heart. The second discovery is to notice that the attachment is a desire inside the person and a habit created by one's conditioning. Finally by simply being sensitive the person can see that anxiety is a by-product of this attachment-desire. Is the anxiety level worth the particular worldly prize that is being coveted? Attachments actually control a person.

Two approaches a person might choose when infatuated or totally absorbed by a particular possession, accomplishment, ideal or person are described below.

First, there is the admission of disappointment since an obsession is unsatisfying and a waste of one's life. Second, the presence of God's Grace enables the retreatant to discover the unchanging nature of God's love and realize that every attachment is in the mind, not in reality.

To discover that there is no loss in reality is quite shocking and enormously liberating. When there is no powerful inclination or inordinate attachment, there is the courage and the ability to choose. You no longer submit to slavery or lose your freedom to the motives of profit, success or achievement. There is no clinging to false promises of salvation or security, for you have a deep sense that you are alive now, already loved and certainly saved. There is no longer an inward discouragement but even a clear outward thrust. God's will is being fulfilled in you and by you in whatever choice you make. God's care for God's people is seen in their service to each other. This kind of love casts out all attachments.

17. MUTUAL TRUST

When the director is accompanying a retreatant he ought not to investigate the past or the failures of the retreatant or strive to know his private thoughts, for the relationship of the retreatant is specifically with the Lord who already knows one's past successes and failures, thoughts and desires. However, during the retreat time it will be very helpful if the thoughts and disturbances that occur in the present are willingly shared with the director. If they are causing anxieties, fears, joys or sorrows, they will be helpful to the spiritual director as he proposes spiritual exercises in accordance with the disposition of the retreatant. The director will also be able to evaluate the progress being made so that suitable exercises can be adapted to the needs of the person. This relationship involves caring without curiosity, sharing without confession, openness without obligation, and vulnerability without gullibility. There is an ongoing communication and trust in the relationship.

18. ADAPTING THE EXERCISES

The Spiritual Exercises must be adapted to the condition of the one who is to engage in them, taking into consideration one's age, physical stamina, education, special talents and degree of interest in theology and spirituality. Once these qualities are evaluated, the exercises which would be most helpful are explained and proposed to the retreatant. The retreatant would then express the extent of his willingness to dispose himself for them and determine which exercises seem most appealing.

In the past some retreat directors and retreatants were under the impression that some stress and strain ought to accompany these exercises, that the retreatant should adapt to the structure rather than the reverse. The emphasis was placed on sacrifice, discipline and conformity rather than on consolation, celebration and discovery.

A critical point in assigning exercises of such a spiritual type is choosing exercises that are not only worthwhile but enjoyable. The prayer itself should not be an obstacle or a hardship, but rather a very productive and beneficial experience. Exercises in which the retreatant and the retreat director can sense the benefit derived, provide mutually discernible progress and indicate the proper choice for further exercises.

Ignatius gives some suggestions on essential topics to be included for those who do not wish to make the entire thirty day retreat in depth. The fruit can be derived from these exercises with some special instruction and with key meditations adapted to the person's situation. Discernibly, if one attains peace of soul, it is a clear sign that he is benefiting from these exercises.

Two required exercises are the Particular Examen and the General Examen which are presented in detail in Annotations # 24 - 43. Also required are clarifications regarding prayer time, one's commitments, and the typical inclinations that may dissuade a person from believing in himself. The two basic Commandments that are written on our hearts and the specific Scriptures that tell the wondrous story of salvation are critical themes for this restricted style of retreat. If the retreatant is living away from the actual premises, weekly or regular interviews with the director and frequent reception of the Eucharist are recommended.

For those who are unable to make the Exercises in their entirety, there are five topics that Ignatius recommends for the director to discuss fully with the retreatant: the Commandments, the capital sins, the five senses, the works of mercy and the precepts of the church. These considerations will provide the basic themes for the retreatant's prayer, with meaningful applications for one's life. They will also prove to be most profitable for the individual in his daily imitation of Christ. (# 238 - 248)

In examining the strength and aptitude of the retreatant, the director has interesting decisions to make regarding his expectations of what will be most nourishing and bear the most fruit. The retreatant needs to examine his own awareness of himself and provide some feedback, so that in mutual understanding the director will be able to propose some guidelines that will facilitate the retreat.

Ignatius encouraged meeting consistently. Essential to this regular encounter is flexibility in selecting a convenient time for the sessions, with specific length and frequency. When a particular meeting or the other's presence is desired and appreciated, explaining awareness exercises and proposing spiritual exercises is easy for the director and profitable for the retreatant. When this is followed, good effects will be noticed. For example, when a community shares freely and joyfully, the gathering becomes a true service and the people become the Eucharist. There is natural consolation.

While confession has been a custom during traditional retreats, sharing the results of past experiences within the Sacrament of Reconciliation will be of added benefit during retreat most appropriately with someone other than the director.

19. THE NINETEENTH ANNOTATION AT HOME RETREAT

This is especially for those who are busy about public affairs and other necessary occupations.

The meditations that are central to these abbreviated exercises include: First, a logical meditation on creation, specifically ourselves as creatures. This provides a strong foundation for our belief that a loving God gave us life, that we are heirs, that we are miraculously images of God and have a significant role in the world. Second, the particular and general examination of consciousness are presented so that the retreatant can use these awareness exercises effectively. Following this, a determination regarding confession, its place and purpose on this retreat ought to be discussed.

For approximately three of the days it is important to meditate on the world's most common illusions and our society's habitual blindness. Just as a corporation cannot think, neither can society; it has no mind. A herd of animals is led by a leader who is amazed that others follow. We are living in a world that is insensitive and blind. The corporate, institutional and national propensity for survival perpetuates insensitivity and greed on a large scale.

The sin of the world is my sin. My own blindness and ignorance cause me to live in a multitude of illusions that block my vision of reality. My natural sensitivity and compassionate responses are dulled.

Ignatius thinks it is extremely important that we see the results of the world's blindness in order to be motivated to break through our own illusions. It is important to see the damage that has been caused by misconceptions and biases, by neglecting to take the care to find the truth. It is revealing to see the results of hardness and righteousness, and to witness the unwillingness or inability to see people as people. There is a tendency to judge people by conceptual norms and labels rather than to accept them as unique individuals. Look at the violence resulting from ignorance, blindness and judgment. Understanding our own blindness will make us more patient in accepting the mistakes of the world.

During this "19th Annotation", the mysteries of the life of Christ keep before our minds the example of One Whose eyes were open, Whose heart was sensitive, and Whose actions were replete with courage and generosity.

Ignatius recommends one hour and a half of daily spiritual exercises for the duration of the retreat. The indicated time ought not be a stumbling block; it is not restricted to one sitting, nor is it an ideal or a rule. It simply worked for many people. What is satisfactory for each retreatant needs to be explored. It would be self-defeating if the person who was making a retreat felt discouraged, guilty or inadequate because of prayer, yet it can and does happen. The actual sense of consolation during prayer can be flattened by the expectation of a certain amount of minutes or seconds for prayer. We live in a passing world, so the notion of quantity of time is impossible to avoid. However, if we measure our prayer not by time, but by some personal interior meaning, this common obstacle will be overcome. It is very helpful when the framework of the exercises is constantly adjusted to the nature of the retreatant.

Ignatius suggests that the Additions in Annotations # 73 - 89 be explained at this time as they will be helpful for one's private prayer.

20. PREREQUISITES FOR THE LONG RETREAT

The Spiritual Exercises in their totality are for persons who are capable of being disengaged from their normal demands, occupations, involvements and concerns. These people are able to give themselves on a daily and complete basis to these exercises. Obviously a secluded place of retreat would be most suited for such an endeavor. Then the order of meditations can be followed as presented in these pages, and the retreatant will have time for three to five meditations per day with two examens.

Ignatius implies that the experience of the exercises can be more powerful if the retreatant is able to withdraw "from all friends and acquaintances and from all worldly cares" or if he can "conveniently withdraw from the place where he is residing." This detachment from concerns and worries is essential for making progress. Some people are able to withdraw physically to make a retreat but are unable to detach themselves from their psychological burdens. The degree of attachment or distraction could become an impediment. This should be determined by the retreatant and the director prior to the retreat.

Certain important factors for a good retreat need to be discussed and clarified. They include each one's previous expectations of the retreat experience, the most appropriate times and places for meditation, the degree of freedom and flexibility that is permitted and any particulars that will facilitate rapport with the director.

When Ignatius made his thirty day retreat at Manresa, he was left on his own. He had the opportunity to experience a noncompetitive atmosphere, freedom of movement, a non-regimented life style, and unimpaired individuality of expression. The place where you plan to make retreat should have as few restrictions as possible. The freedom of the children of God will be experienced better in an open setting with accepting people.

The availability of a quiet place, prayerful people and participation at the Eucharist can be most helpful. The availability of a natural or rugged landscape and a secluded location are also conducive but not essential. Mountains, valleys and bodies of water provide exquisite settings.

St Ignatius mentions three particular advantages to separating from worldly cares.

First, by cutting the ties from friends and familiar settings, one reveals the degree of commitment, the clarity of intention and the strength of resolve to make a good retreat. It also is a letting go of the normal demands of a personal, family, apostolic or business nature that can easily fill the day. The detachment process starts when one decides to begin a journey, then makes the arrangements, and finally when one says "goodbye".

Second, if a person is less involved with mundane responsibilities he will have more opportunity to devote himself to discoveries of a different nature. To reflect on feelings and have time to examine their causes can totally change one's responses.

It is a unique opportunity to grow in awareness. Much of life is not even seen, no less understood and many experiences and people go unappreciated. Giving attention and allotting time to ponder these exterior and interior discoveries lead to maturity and greater joy.

Third, in freely getting away, one can relish one's unity with the world and with God, and realize an integrity within oneself. This brings a realization that one is filled with grace and surrounded by grace. Withdrawing from preoccupations and obligations enables the retreatant to be aware of being singularly gifted. Wherever one is or whatever one does, God's presence, invitation and favor precede him. Being alone could be threatening for some people, but by choosing to be alone on retreat, one loses all sense of fear and finds many ways of sensing the presence of God.

21. SPIRITUAL EXERCISES

The first purpose of this series of exercises is to feel a pervading peace. When we realize that we are loved and favored by God, we will live with an imperturbable confidence each day, in every decision that we make. This trust and self-assurance prevents us from being harried, compulsive or greedy. The effects will be obvious to every person we meet. As we go about our lives there will be an intelligent pace and a sensitivity to all of life that make a person's reactions appropriately compassionate. This flavors our peace with joy.

The second purpose of the Exercises is to gain a proper perspective regarding life after one leaves the security of the retreat. We should try to use the fruits gained during that peaceful time to objectively evaluate our life and gradually amend it if necessary. If we discover that we have made gods out of attachments or power, we can look to Jesus, who imitated no one and who clung to nothing, not even to being God. It is important that we recognize and avoid judgments against ourselves and others, and always choose Christ's way of transformation, acceptance.

The third purpose of these exercises is to be able to find God in all things, everywhere, in everyone - to go forth with the peace of Christ, the presence of God and in harmony with creation.

22. PRESUPPOSITION

Since the retreatant will be working with another person during the exercises, it is important to cooperate with and benefit from each other. One of the simplest aids to communication and understanding is the ability and desire to put a good interpretation on another's statement, rather than focusing on its limitations, or even attempting to be objective. Frequently, a valid reason for the statement or behavior can be seen, but if not, it is good to ask how the person understands it. What is the positive value or the truth that one can perceive in this statement? Asking for clarification is helpful for communication. People often repeat what others say without examining it for themselves. The opinions of others can short circuit our experiencing, even our own seeing. By expressing interest, by asking questions, by caring, it is easy to come to the intention and the actual meaning of another's views.

Often when there is inaccuracy in the communication of ideas it is due to secondhand information. People are so conditioned that often they do not speak what they themselves have seen and believed. However, if people are patient and trusting, they can come to an understanding of the facts by inquiring about the firsthand sources.

When we are in the process of dropping illusions and attachments, it is important to understand that the conditioning and prejudiced thoughts that we bring from our background are not our own. We have no need to be defensive about our conditioning, whether it is familial, religious or patriotic. This understanding helps in overcoming the powerful influences that interfere with our growth in wisdom and sensitivity.

Ignatius calls this disposition of looking for the good interpretation in another's statement: "presupposition". It is an initial starting point for honest communication between retreatant and director.

As we are involved in the process of finding God and good in all things, it is essential that in the relationship between the director and the retreatant a tangible discovery of good is revealed in actions, words and intentions.

23. FIRST PRINCIPAL AND FOUNDATION

When Jesus was asked what it meant to love and serve God,

He answered, "Love the neighbor that you do see". On another occasion He said, "Love one another as I have loved you". Then He gave us the example of washing people's feet, spending time with the poor, accepting the rejected and welcoming the condemned. His example was very clear. At another time Jesus said, "Show your love for God by showing love for each other". The meaning was evident to those who had ears to hear; it is still heart warming to people of goodwill today.

Persons are created to praise, reverence and serve God our Lord and by this means to save their souls. Salvation means to be secure, satisfied and happy, to have a full heart and a lively spirit, to be without internal conflict, like a loved child. This is what Jesus meant by "Become like a child". This is what heaven is. This is what it means to be redeemed, or to save one's soul. Salvation is not something that you do or that will only happen after death, or something that has not been seen before. Neither is it anything for which people should fight, kill or die.

The kingdom of God is here; we have been created to discover it in peace, in harmony and in community. God has created us to see and find God in everyone, everywhere. When we do find God, we find ourselves reverencing life for we sense the goodness so clearly in each being. This awareness of God's presence causes two things to happen: First, it brings a deep sense of consolation and joy and second, it gives us the impetus and strength to serve in any way we can with ease and compassion. This service becomes a joy like no other and it becomes the nourishment of our life. It is a kingdom without fear and without manipulation, a kingdom whose only power is one of love. It is ours, it is here; it is the purpose for which we have been created. This is what God has provided for us.

When we look at the tapestry of life and realize that God has conceived it all to help us attain happiness and harmony, it seems such a lovely plan. We need to choose the strands that will bring about happiness most readily. We need to discover and avoid the ones that do not work. It is still a surprise that the use of God's gifts could ever lead to conflict, confusion, anxiety, and desolation. God has given us intellect to sort things out, common sense to evaluate and hearts to enjoy these things. "Taste and see," Jesus said. Our God-given vocation is to cooperate for the peace of the world, and to make decisions to achieve this end.

Basically, we need to determine what things will help us in the attainment of our end and which things we must say 'no' to, or rid ourselves of, so that they do not prove to be a hindrance. Our yeses and nos, our trials and errors help us to discover which ones are constructive for God's people and which ones are not.

Once I have a clear sense of which is a hindrance and which is a help, my response will be accurate. Becoming "indifferent" or particularly objective, will be of great assistance. Throughout my life, I have formed preferences, biases and attachments. Ignatius is proposing that I remain as honest as possible in discovering my biases that do not help me in my search for God. The word "indifference" means the ability to see all things and myself as good. It enables me to see many choices in life that are conducive to what I really wish to attain. Does this thrust really bring satisfaction and joy? Does it lead me to reverence and praise? Does it lead me to serve?

I examine my life with this litmus test, specifically my concerns about health or sickness, riches or poverty, honor or dishonor, a long life or a short life. I notice whether I am attached, greedy or anxious about any of these things.

The first clue that there might be a problem is fear. If I prefer one of these things, do I have a fear of losing it? These preferences seem like they are normal, but if I am influenced by fear I am not truly free. The value of indifference is realized when my fear subsides, when I realize that I am no longer controlled by my preferences. I will now be open to finding God even in bad times - sickness, rejection and poverty. So too for all other things.

The second indication of a serious attachment is greed. When life, things and people are not seen as they are and as they were created, the desire to have more becomes insatiable and the tendency to abuse them is unleashed. People then crave ever greater honors, longer lives and better reputations. The greed becomes a block to basic harmony. The appetite for more land, money, power and prestige destroys one's taste for life and peace. The good spirit that nourishes and satisfies the heart becomes unappealing. If there is to be a choice it needs to be for whatever is more conducive to the end for which we are created. Be open to the possibility that there are other ways that might be more effective. The constant theme expressed in the Principle and Foundation is an indifference that brings happiness through freedom and detachment. There is special joy in experiencing these exercises and in achieving the goal of each contemplation. Praise of God, reverence for life, and service of people bring lasting delight to the soul.

THE FIRST WEEK

24. THE DAILY PARTICULAR EXAMEN

SELECTIVE AWARENESS. The awareness that one is "on retreat" affects one's thoughts, words and actions. Ignatius suggests beginning the morning with the recollection that the retreatant is doing something very special, by living this day, by responding to God's call, by taking time for retreat. It is sobering and celebrating, reflective and personal. The purpose of this examen is to enhance the meaning of ordinary life through selective awareness. During each day there is a particular grace or goal on which the retreatant is focusing. It may be a certain illusion, obstacle, or inordinate attachment that the person is trying to understand more clearly and react to with more wisdom.

25. AFTERNOON

Ignatius asks the retreatant to recall the grace he desires and to ask the Lord again for this grace. In this brief examen, there is a particular point from the morning's prayer that might be recalled. It might simply be the grace to become more fully aware. We can easily become immersed and bogged down by minutiae. We look at the events that transpired since rising and notice if there were some opportunities that were not responded to for one reason or another. The particular message of this day needs to be renewed. We renew our resolution to respond more wholeheartedly during the rest of the day. If we have been performing appropriately we might just give thanks.

26. EVENING

At night there is another examen. Become aware of the numerous opportunities that were presented during the day. See if you notice some growth. How difficult it is to de-condition yourself, even while you are identifying the specific hindrances to a loving and worry-free life!

This examen is helpful for learning a new language, one of good news, one that is spirit-filled. We are shaping our lives the way we wish to shape them. We become the masters of our lives instead of submitting to a known or unknown authority, a type of critical parent, that has scolded us when we did not conform to its prejudiced dictates. Obligations that had provided a sense of security and direction while we were young must be reassessed.

Living in a continual state of awareness, we are experiencing feelings more clearly. When we worry we are able to catch our fears and calmly trace their origins. We are centers, not just moving into action, but reflecting while we are in action. We are self-sufficient, no longer needing to wait for the report card of approval to determine how well we are performing.

FOUR ADDITIONAL DIRECTIONS

27. PROCESS

A person who is in touch with his center does not need to wait for the next examen to see if the day has progressed satisfactorily. For example, if I am deliberating on my need for approval and the impact of rejection and criticism, I do not need to wait for the next examen to be aware that I felt rejected during the day. Sometimes I seem in charge while it is happening; at other times I am helpless in this new situation. Creative behavior, like new insights can be life-giving. The examen is a careful review which provides new approaches to whatever I am focused on for that day.

28. CLARITY

Can the retreatant notice any improvement from one examen to the next? Breaking through the illusions of my life occurs in daily increments. Seeing the need and the problem takes a moment; exercising for growth and strength takes a lifetime. This examen approach, even with simple things, requires a constant and direct focus.

29. TOLERANCE

Ignatius recommends that various comparisons be made during the examen periods to help evaluate the degree of improvement. Am I finding my own joy in life or am I dependent on others? The examen has two purposes: to encourage the person and to make him more aware. I come to a heightened awareness when I realize I am loved unconditionally by God. The belief that it is unnecessary and impossible to earn God's love puts me at ease. There is a greater joy and freedom in making use of my time and my talents. When I am not threatened I can live my life and use my gifts in a healthy and constructive way.

30. PERSEVERANCE
Just as you are encouraged to compare one examen with another, compare one week's examen with that of the previous week. How have you grown?

31. NOTE
Ignatius suggests coming up with a schedule that keeps records of the things you have already completed and a list of topics for future examens, just as you need reminders to help with daily appointments.

GENERAL EXAMINATION OF CONSCIOUSNESS

32. VALUE
The purpose of a General Examen, Ignatius wrote, is to purify the soul. He loved to be introspective, loved to figure out the way the mind functioned and how thoughts originate. Ignatius passed on this rewarding process as a gift to future retreatants.

There are three types of thoughts. The first type arises from within me, from my free will. The second kind of thought concerns the good of others. As I observe the needs of people, I consider ways to help them have a better life. Ignatius would sometimes call thoughts of doing good for God's people "the good spirit" (i.e. God's praise and service). The third comes from seeing society and desiring more things: material goods, lofty positions and worldly power.

When I take time to silently observe myself, my actions and the world, it is valuable to determine whether inspiration is the source of my thoughts or if something external is drawing me.

When thoughts are accompanied by ardent desires a powerful force called ambition is born. In striving for transient achievements, basic human joy can be replaced with the need for thrills. The thought that I am deprived or inadequate is depressing and leads to desperate behavior. Attitudes of jealousy and envy, for example, would reveal that I am not content with my life. My actions may be for the service of others yet my thoughts may be obsessed with comparison.

These sundry types of thoughts, as Ignatius called them may be difficult to isolate but understanding them will be very fruitful and worth every examen.

33. THOUGHTS

When people see clearly, they do not have temptations to misuse things or have any craving to possess them.

When they see how hot the fire is they have absolutely no desire to touch it. Once they discover that these desires are not of God choosing becomes elementary. Those who have come through detachment to awareness are a light to the world. A person who has wisdom, compassion and tolerance has the grace for directing people without getting in their way. He has the ability to see the apparent goods and the illusions of this world without rejecting them. The aware person has the advantage of understanding firsthand what people experience. He can understand how people can be enticed. When people are not awake they are living in a dream world obsessed by prestige, success, wealth, power and pride.

34. SELF-POSSESSED

Each time you find the strength to be master of your life in spite of the influences of the world, precious rewards of happiness and freedom ensue. To avoid being ruled by the habits of the past, the seductions of one's surroundings or society's approbation is a very special kind of conquering of self. Sometimes the pressures are great for those who have been affected by strict doctrine, the fear of God, or a repressive environment. This could also be the case with an addictive personality or with a person who lives in a dysfunctional relationship.

35. THINK FOR YOURSELF

Ignatius wants the retreatant to be extremely honest in admitting where there is still some residue of previous conditioning that weighs him down or distracts him. A person who finds war glamorous, believes that authority has the answer for his life, or feels that success and achievement will make him happy is a fine example of the influence of conditioning.

Rewards were offered to many innocent youths who sacrificed their early years or their lives. Young people were told, "If you do what we tell you, you can become heroes". Some young religious aspirants were told, "If you do what we tell you, you shall see God." By what promises and illusions are you living that prevent you from experiencing life? Why would any healthy per-

son want to surrender his God-given will to another, to a constitution or to an authority figure?

No one who has seen victims and devastation could see any
value in the use of violence and fear. Only the person who has
been drugged or indoctrinated could not see the cruelty. It is
important to admit that there is a lure in drugs, a thrill in winning,
a security in power, and pride in being considered a hero. These
are serious epidemics of worldwide proportions; they affect
countries and churches. The glamour of military violence in
every nation still exists. The torture of humanity through the
ages has been promoted by a deceptive bias, "our side". The
essence of the lie is that it denies that God is the Creator of all -
there are no "sides" with God.

If one is taking pleasure in the control or manipulation of individuals, he will only wake up when the authority who initially
programmed him has a change of heart. Only when the master
pushes new buttons can the robot function differently. Ignatius
wants us to realize how susceptible people are. He wants to
make sure we keep alert and avoid the inclination to surrender
ourselves to any master, regardless of its glamour and power.

36. LISTEN TO YOUR INSPIRATIONS

We are created to love our neighbor as ourselves. Only those
who feel they have been deprived of love can wish harm to their
neighbor. Ignatius gives some guidelines for reflecting about
destructive activity. Ask this question, "Would we want to perform a destructive act if the opportunity arose?" If the answer
is "yes" then something is wrong with our view of life; we are
not awake, and certainly not aware of God's plan for us. This
evil intention can only come from misunderstanding and ignorance. It is violent and can develop an attitude toward creatures
that is divisive and debilitating. When people are violent to others they are reacting to violence within themselves or to an earlier repressive formation. Both indicate internal conflicts.

Peace begins in one's heart. It is against our nature to be cruel
or to accept cruelty, to harm or to be harmed. Yet particular
goals, ideals or rewards have the power to blind us. To be
Christlike means to see. It means preferring to be rejected oneself rather than to harm another. For a healthy, reflective
Christian to be a soldier involves frequent contradictions.

Unfortunately, because of evildoers peace keeping forces are necessary. The intention or willingness to destroy others violates the essentials of living. Just as actions of love express unity and come from a full heart, so acts of violence spread disunity and reveal a destitute heart.

37. REFLECTIVE BEHAVIOR

Carrying out violent actions is one step worse than harboring violent thoughts. While one is considering destructive acts there is still time to repent and reject the path of violence. At times actions cause more damage than words because the rebuilding and reconstruction phase is longer, more painful and affects more of God's people. If people can initiate negotiation and dialogue when confronted with evil they can avoid the spread of violence. When these gifts are implemented, there is no greater joy. Blessed are the peacemakers!

38. WORDS

We are the work of God's loving design, so to hate another is inappropriate. A curse means to ask God to bring harm to another. Since God is the God of all, it would be an empty gesture.

Only to protect a life do we need to swear to convince people that we are telling the truth. In serious matters it enables us to get peoples' attention. If they are distracted by bribes, influence and prestige, they are reminded when a person swears that this is God's world and we are His people. When the truth is not evident or obvious, then it is appropriate to call on God. But normally to call on God to confirm one's word trivializes the name of God. We are one with the truth when we live it as well as speak it.

In our examination of conscience, notice the words we use in referring to each person. Ignatius says swearing is to be done with reverence. Our words are not just signs of interior meaning, but bonds of our unity with one another and God.

God is not more present in one being than in another. It is unnecessary to impress those who believe they are children of the same loving God with the use of God's name for they are witnesses to God themselves. By calling on God in the presence of evil-doers or with indoctrinated persons, those who do not believe will be unimpressed by any profession of faith.

It is common behavior to categorize people by their affiliation to a certain ethnic, political or religious group, rather than to see each as a uniquely loved person. We show our love for God by honoring, respecting and reverencing our neighbor.

39. LET YOUR WORDS BE TRUE

People who are meditative and who seek the presence of God in all things would naturally be more responsive to others. Those who have been treated with love and kindness have had the best teachers in the ways of the kingdom. They would certainly be less apt to manipulate others according to their designs. They would not misuse lovely phrases like "the will of God" or impose their will on others while using terminology like "for God and country." Neither would they bind people under obedience and imply that they now had an obligation to God. They would be more careful because they know the superstitious tendencies and the gullibility of human beings. They will be careful not to use statements like "you owe it to God" or "you should" or "it is the right thing". For the young and innocent will not understand the nuances of these clichés. The unsophisticated will be threatened by any authority using divine words or invoking some tradition as if it were equated with the truth. And so those in places of responsibility ought to be careful not to swear in order to coerce, but simply tell the truth and let the truth be heard.

Of prime concern during the examen are the illusions that we live by and the doctrines of others that sway us from the truth. It is idolatry to revere material things and beliefs more than people. It is a modern form of idolatry to be obsessed by isms and ideals, rather than being sensitive to life and relating to others with compassion. Another form of idolatry is to crave success or the accumulation of honors and wealth, which interferes with true happiness. Fear is yet another form of idolatry. To fear others means that we mistrust God's people; to fear the future displays a lack of confidence in God's providence. Another dangerous illusion is righteousness, the idealization of one's opinion and the disdain or condemnation of others. For our conditioned tendencies appear to be appropriate but they actually interfere with true happiness.

If we can find God in all things, we will live without fear or obligation because His presence is freeing. God, who shared all things with us, delivers us from the need and the greed to accumulate. To see beyond those illusions can bring great joy and God's peace.

40. HEAR WHAT YOU SAY

As part of the retreat, Ignatius wants us to reflect on the words that we typically exchange with others. Can we sense the intention and the effect of our words? Do our words bring joy, peace or encouragement? Are our words appreciative and sharing, constructive and kind?

Maybe our words are mechanical or habitual.

It is possible that our words are not living expressions but merely repetitions from a previous environment. Are our words good news? Certain expressions, as if from free association or compulsion, seem to flow without relevant thoughtfulness or positive meaning. Other phrases, without intending to be destructive, reveal the unspirited use of our mind and mouth.

41. COURAGEOUS INTERVENTION

Ignatius exhorts the retreatant to exemplify the gospel mandate to return good for evil. Being aware of the harm that people do, take even more care not to return evil for evil. Our actions reveal our own weaknesses and strengths. When we speak about another's limitations we need to take great care, because in doing so we reveal our own biases, our own obsessions and our own willingness to condemn. To be a person of peace, one must be able to bring sanctuary to people who are threatened and fearful, and a sense of security to people who are deprived. In an attempt to enforce justice people often create havoc. It is so difficult to be a mediator without interfering in people's lives.

Justice is a lovely term though it implies judgment. It is always subjective and therefore easily abused since it is meted out by individuals who have their own notion of justice. Working for peace and justice is a burdensome vocation, for taking care of oneself is difficult enough.

How does one work toward peace without condemning the individuals that seem to perpetuate the violence? It requires a special grace to be able to see both sides of a controversy, to empathize with people who are enemies, the persecutors as well as the victims.

Ignatius gives two occasions when it is advisable to speak of the faults of others. The first is when the knowledge and understanding of the offense will assist the community. Further inquiry ought to be made prior to accepting the initial description of the action. The context must be seen as a whole, with an effort to understand the reasons why such behavior might have occurred. The violation must be public and shameless to a person of common sense.

The second occasion when it is good to talk about the damage caused is when there is a chance to really help the person and the situation. When someone is capable of helping another and there is probable grounds that assistance will be effective, initiative is warranted. The intention then is never to spread scandal, but to support and correct when possible.

42. DEEDS

Ignatius highly recommends a thorough examination of one's life as it conforms to the Ten Commandments and to the special laws of the church. He also encourages retreatants to be attentive to those in authority who are caring, capable and enlightened.

Following the Ten Commandments brings harmony to the community and to one's personal life. By reverencing other people, the neighbor's goods and another's reputation, we enhance them in word and action. Being mindful that God is our Father and we are His revered holy family, we preserve respect for ourselves and for the members of this worldwide family. By living according to the Commandments, by keeping in close touch with the secular community, we can be conscientious and caring as well as knowledgeable. We are able to see all people as God's children.

Besides the basic commandments, there are special guidelines in word and deed that have helped bring about a greater peace for the world: inspiring encyclicals written by spiritual leaders, direct service groups such as Amnesty International, Maryknoll, the Red Cross, The United Nations and Catholic Relief Services. They know what is necessary to live in peace, for they have seen the deprivation throughout the world and the hunger for equality and for basic human rights. The purpose of every just law is to bring harmony and to foster peace. Forgiveness, amnesty and acceptance are the first steps to true peace. The

Eucharist, the meal of unity, is a celebration of the awareness of our need for each other and of the promise to help one another. It is an awesome reminder that encourages people to come to the table and break bread together, so that this sacrament of unity may effect what it signifies. And so, whatever we can do by our presence, our words and our actions are the deeds of the kingdom. This is our great privilege and our vocation, to imitate Christ.

43. THE FIVE STEP METHOD OF EXAMEN

Here is a method for using the general examination of conscience.

First, remember to give thanks for favors received in the past. Appreciation is a specifically human attribute. The secret to appreciation is to realize how uniquely you have been gifted.

Second, ask for the grace to see your illusions. What in particular seems to put limits on your free response to God's grace? Do the obstacles occur primarily through ideas, people or possessions?

Third, since your last examination have you been realistic about your thoughts, goals, frustrations? Did you stay in touch with your inner life and desires? Review your communication and silence with others, the development of new relationships and the decline of others. Look at your activities as they involve your degree of involvement and the use of things.

Fourth, realize God's presence in your day: how you have been taken care of and the opportunities for goodness that God offered you this day.

Fifth, have you made any discoveries? Did you experience gratitude or sorrow? Have you uncovered some of your illusions?

Close this examination with an Our Father.

44. GENERAL CONFESSION

During this graced time of retreat a general confession would be helpful as a reminder of God's unconditional acceptance and as a clear sign of God's providence throughout your past life.

Those who constantly respond to present opportunities and who find the living God in each day might require a special effort to look at the past. They would need to have the same context as existed in the past - which is impossible. The past is gone and exists only as a biased recollection. Yet some understanding of former patterns of behavior can be helpful in discovering better ways of responding in the present. While there is no obligation to make a general confession, during the time of retreat there may be a greater experience of love and a helpful objectivity regarding one's limitations.

Another reason for "Reconciliation" is that sometimes we can discover the basic direction of our lives when we see our personal history from a new perspective. We may discover some basic misdirections or some long-standing illusions. This can lead to greater appreciation and spiritual growth. This provides a deep sense of humility, clarity and understanding comparable to the Fifth step of the famous "Twelve Step Programs." The consequences are trust in God, a feeling of inner strength, and courage for future actions.

Ignatius suggests making this general confession after the exercises of the First Week, i.e. after Annotation # 100.

MEDITATIONS ON SIN

45. FIRST EXERCISE

In this first exercise three aspects of sin will be presented. Ignatius recommends the three powers of the soul, namely, "the memory, understanding and will" be applied to each consideration. He mentions that essential to each of the following Exercises is a preparatory prayer and then two special preludes. The three main points for the meditation are followed by an intimate colloquy. These comprise the ingredients that he recommends for each of these meditations.

46. PREPARATORY PRAYER

The retreatant asks God for the grace that intentions, actions, and operations will be directed to the praise and service of the Divine Majesty. This is a simple and humble prayer, for everything that we have belongs to God, everything that we do is because of God, and everything that we are is for the praise of God. So this is a brief prayer that reminds us who we are in the presence of God.

47. FIRST PRELUDE

This is to conceive of a mental representation, called composition of place, to coincide with our prayer.

Sometimes our meditation might include an image of a moun-
tainside, seaside, or crowd of people. These or other scenes may
be helpful as we construct and control the fantasy. Composing a
place is especially helpful when meditating on something that is
less visible, like the feeling of rejection. To imagine ourselves in
a refugee camp, in prison for our political convictions, or silenced
because of our spiritual insights might present the desired milieu
for a meditation on rejection or abandonment. These kinds of
images provide an appropriate mood if I am to consider ideas that
require my complete attention and sensitivity.

48. SECOND PRELUDE

It is revealing to discover what I desire. What is close to my
heart? Am I in touch with my inner self? To answer these mysterious questions, Ignatius suggests directing them to God. By
taking the time to listen to what is deep within me, I am able
to sift out what is important.

Although we often have intentions for our prayer, the particular petition for this prelude should be consistent with the subject
matter. If I were meditating on Jesus' passion, some appealing
graces might include: the desire to understand what people give
their lives for, to understand the love of Christ, or possibly to find
a way to be patient in crises. When meditating on the
Resurrection, I might ask for the grace to understand what this
kingdom of God means or to experience is some way the reunion
of Jesus with His Father.

We can make a difference if we see how the world has failed to
secure a lasting peace and sometimes our own decisions have not
brought peace to the situation at work or at home. According to
our power and position we have the ability to bring life or destroy
it. It is shocking to see how one government authority or one religious leader can cause such widespread suffering and loss of
lives, sometimes affecting entire nations. This realization may
lead us to ask for the grace of clarity about our own limitations
as well as an understanding about the power we have to affect situations. We may desire the grace to wake up, see the mess and
do something about it. Understanding God's power working in

us can bring about significant changes, helping us renew the face of the earth in our little quadrant.

49. NOTE

Ignatius makes special mention that at the beginning of prayer, a preparatory prayer should always be said. It brings to consciousness the purpose of our life, the purpose of our day, and a specific reminder that this prayer is God's gift. It is a singularly important centering moment. Also the first prelude gives us a few moments to imagine the place that I am in or about which I am meditating. This picturing of place gives some control to the usual distractions in life that make demands on our time and thoughts and that usually dissipate some of our energy. The second prelude's purpose is to take a few moments to rediscover my own desires which need to surface. This gives a sense of humility and honesty to my prayer as I start the particular meditation.

50. FIRST POINT

Look at the nature of sin and come up with your own conclusions from these observations. What do you think was the first sin in your life? How does an error or mistake become labeled a sin? It is important to understand this from your memory of what others have taught and from what you have believed about it. Your own experience and personal patterns of behavior are most relevant.

What actually does cause sin? We are examining here the nature and source of evil and the judgments implied. Do you believe that God has made all things good from the smallest to the greatest, from the beginning of time to the end, from every facet of life to every thought and action in every person? If God is the creator, where does evil come from? How does one accurately judge something as evil and then describe it as sinful? Does a committee, or do you have the power to give the label "evil" or the additional title "sin" to things that are subjectively perceived as evil?

What is this evil or sin? Who judges it? Who names it? There are no short answers, for throughout the world many accuse others of sin. We have been taught to condemn evil without getting to the source, maybe just using the terminology without much reflection. We know that most people are repulsed and influenced by the terms evil, evil spirit, sin or sinful.

Would you describe sin as an action that disregards your own best interest or that violates the dignity of a human being? To reject the freedom that God has given you would be a shame. To act against your own will and grace is a waste of a life, is it not?

If you do not follow your heart there is disharmony, for you are acting in a manner that is not truly yours. Some explanation and further reflection may help. Go at your own pace, take your time. There are some apparent contradictions that require your own evaluation so that you may act with integrity.

Drugs are good for people who are suffering. Rather than condemn people who are on drugs or condemn drugs, how do you determine when it becomes evil and sinful? What is wrong? If the government says it is allowed, is it still wrong? We come once again to the question of evil. How do you define it? Ignatius wants the retreatant to be able to understand, think over in detail, and to recall that we are all created in the state of grace, that we are all free under God, and loved by God from the beginning. How can anyone who is in God and in Christ, as we are, possibly sin? How can there be so much evil and at the same time so much good?

If people are sensitive and know the discomfort of pain, why do people harm one another? Violence is filled with horror and yet it exists in the administrations of so many countries by those who are often called ironically, "security" forces. They are actually large committees who perpetrate internal and external violence. There are experts who are well known and those that are undercover; the stated purpose of both is to enforce the ends of the committee.

Government soldiers wear badges declaring "Follow me" or some other inspirational motto. How distracting! Follow you, to do what? Killing and dying by the bayonet, bullet or bomb? Country upon country is living with this evil; this is the sin of the world. It surrounded Ignatius and he was part of it. It surrounds us and we helplessly support it.

How can we end violence without using violent means or becoming violent ourselves? Jesus was the victim of "Capital Punishment" by church and state. His life, words and final hours give us an example of how to deal with violence.

While people are created to love one another and live in peace, in country after country young people have been convinced to leave family and loved ones to kill others who have the same flesh and spirit, who came from the same Creator, who want only to live in peace and be happy. How can so many on all sides be seduced? What is the attraction of evil, what is the seduction of sin? Where does it originate? Although we are one with God and with each other, we have fallen into disunity and distrust. By distancing people from their loved ones and causing them the pain of loss and separation, we have made them refugees. Who can do this to peace-loving, intelligent people? How can a government that prides itself on being humane do this to its own citizens? Do we ourselves foster violence unknowingly? Was violence done to you?

51. SECOND POINT

Ignatius wants the retreatant to use three levels of understanding. First, use your memory to recall the history of the topic on which you are about to meditate. Second, think it over in detail. Third, enter into the scene with sensitivity.

In trying to discover the origin of sin or the history of evil for example, think of the injustice and inequality in the present world and the vast number of people who have been deprived of their livelihood or separated from their loved ones. As you consider the bleakness of their lives, meditate on the fact that many live and die without human dignity. Picture the suffering in ghettos or rural areas; be aware of the corruption and the deprivation. See what you are feeling and how you are responding; your responsiveness is what indicates whether you are inspired. Stay with your emotions for a while to reinforce the experience of the meditation.

52. THIRD POINT

Evil has invaded the hearths of many families, but especially affected and victimized are third world people, the poor and the neglected. Ignatius wants the retreatant to see his part in this epidemic. He wants him to be aware of how he has actively or passively been helpless, and to realize that he himself is a microcosm of the world he is observing.

While there is great goodness in us, there are many limitations and fears. Ignatius wants us to examine our potential for helping others as well as our propensity for being powerless and helpless. Because of the nature of evil, we can be enticed by rewards in every area of life, from the popular desire to possess material things to the more despicable desire to conquer others. Many world leaders still think that coercion will bring conversions, that accumulation will bring happiness, that war can bring peace. Our lack of understanding of the past causes us to repeat similar damage and mistakes.

Often we act without being aware of our goodness for we have lived so long without being aware of our oneness with God. We have been exquisitely hand made, God made and gifted.

The immediate consequence of not appreciating ourselves is a lack of appreciation for others. How often have we wanted to win or cheered for a victory over others? How often have we feared losing or felt anxious about a loss? O, we of little faith! Who took away the innocence of our childhood in the name of ambition? Who taught us such small-minded pride? Where were we motivated to outdo our friends, to compete and compare, to be better than others, to achieve more than anyone else and to strive to be above the rest?

What is it that takes away peace and that brings violence into relationships? How often are we in touch with the deep feelings that come from our oneness and our goodness? We have been sent into the world with a finite body and mind, so that we would not see our infinite goodness but accept being ourselves. Since we do not believe who we are, we desire and try to be more than what God has made us to be.

What is the sin of the world?

This meditation has three points with enough material for more than a single meditation. Use the preparatory prayer each time with the representation of place and the specification of grace.

Frequently the grace will be the awareness of how I have lived under illusions, and rather than search for the truth, I reacted automatically. I have been misled and somehow it persisted for too long. Can I see the confusion that has resulted from my illusions? I ask that I may see more clearly and respond more fully out of love.

53. COLLOQUY

In addition to preparing, meditating and responding to the matter for reflection, an integral part of the prayer experience is for the retreatant to have a conversation with Jesus. Imagine for a few moments Christ our Lord present before you. Then

express the feelings, discoveries and the questions that have aris-
en during the prayer period. You might ask questions like the following: If Jesus were in the beginning with God, why would He
want to pass from eternal to mortal life with all the limitations of
being human?

Did Jesus enjoy choosing one good from among the other goods
of the world? How did Jesus feel about the failure and rejection
that He experienced?

It might be good to ask Jesus what He sees in me that He likes
the most. What have I done that is in the likeness of Christ? In
a present context, what am I doing that is like Jesus? How are
my graces and opportunities similar to the ones Jesus had? Ask
Jesus in this colloquy about the future in words such as, "What
would you like me to do today? What would you like me to do
for your people?"

As I have Jesus present in my imagination I ask these questions.
"I wonder why God gives me life! Why did God send me to this
life, and what is God calling me to, before He embraces me
again? What have I done for Christ, and what has Christ done for
me? What do I feel Christ is doing for me now, and what do I feel
I am doing for Christ now? What would I like Christ to do for me
and what would I love to do for Christ?"

54. NOTE ON COLLOQUIES

In this conversational prayer, speak comfortably as one friend
speaks to another - ask for favors or advice, comment on one's
feeling about the other, or describe one's accomplishments and
activities. You could talk about your desires, needs and disappointments; enjoy the sharing as well as the listening. An
important part of the colloquy is to listen to God speak to you
in the depth of your heart and in a variety of mysterious ways.
The colloquy is a very creative and open part of your prayer period, where new creation, new communication and new love is felt
firsthand.

55. SECOND EXERCISE

This is a meditation on my sins. Begin with the preparatory
prayer and the preludes, i.e. a composition of place and a request
for what I desire. Here it will be an awareness of the deep joy
that I was deprived of in the past, what I am missing now and

what I could miss in the future. Since this is a meditation on sin it will be helpful if I examine the many opportunities for doing good or working for peace that I missed.

If the origin of sin is judgment, it seems that an easy way to eliminate sin from the world would be for people to stop judging one another. When have you sinned? People could accuse you of being a sinner, but you may not think that what you did was wrong. Since they judged you as doing something they thought was sinful, they are the ones filled with judgment. Have they not sinned? Do they have any authority to judge others? Does their sin come from their judgment? If you judge yourself as having sinned and someone else does as well, is this judgment correct because two or more have agreed? Could not both be wrong? Does sin come from convictions by others or from self accusations? On what have people based their judgments? If they disagree with what another is saying and doing, do they consider it evil and sinful? Is judgment based on my present standards of what I think is right? Is this the way people banter about the term "sin?"

56. FIRST POINT

Is sin that which causes injury to human life and destruction of property, or is it the misuse of creation? Perhaps it is simply not seeing, like a person who is walking in darkness or in unawareness. Sometimes it is the violation of a law until such time that the law is changed. Then violations would no longer be sins.

What is my record? I review the past according to my personal definition of sin.

I recall the places where I lived, my relationships with people through the years and the different offices I have held. I observe what I failed to do, some of the pain that I caused, and the occasions when I judged others.

57. SECOND POINT

It may be important to weigh the gravity of these aberrations or omissions to see how some have caused misery or have added to the world's woes rather than relieve them. The hurt I have caused is extensive.

It is hard to measure the degree of destruction and pain caused by my fear and ignorance.

When people forget they are God's children they will sin out of self-defense or self-righteousness. They are capable of hurting themselves even while they are attempting to protect themselves. If I do something to defend myself, in the process I may violate others. When there is a powerful sense of loyalty, that ideal becomes more important than human life and God's creatures become mangled in the process. It has been happening for centuries.

58. THIRD POINT

The retreatant needs to be clear about his own personal limitations and about the world's natural fallibility so he experiences no false expectations and no scrupulosity.

The following questions may help. First, who am I compared with all people? I am just one among many; yet one person can do so much. One person with influence can cause other people to sacrifice their lives. Think of one person with influence and what he has done in a few years to cause a trickle down death for so many people.

Second, look down through history at people who have given their lives so others would have a better quality of life.

Third, consider all of creation with its inherent selfish nature in comparison with God, the Creator. I imagine the all-loving God enjoying me just as I am.

Fourth, realize how limited my actions are - at times lethargic, other times unbridled, often compulsive and unreflective. I am a center who is often not centered. I am intelligent and aware, yet so often I am amazed at my incompetence.

Fifth, reflect on how blind I have been, how easily distracted, how oddly motivated. Because of my blindness and ignorance I can be distracted from my own best interest and that of the people I love. It makes me sad to realize how offensive I can be, and it is humbling to be so honest with myself. I desire to treat myself with greater care and accept others graciously, knowing more realistically where judgment comes from.

59. FOURTH POINT

It will be interesting to highlight the differences between darkness and light by setting up the following or similar parallels between wisdom and ignorance, love versus violence, the deep satisfaction of kindness and the anxiety of injustice. Notice the contrast between the haughtiness of righteousness and the beauty of compassion.

Ignatius reminds us that we have not been taught to recognize beauty, but somehow we have been conditioned to evaluate life through the filters of prejudice, insecurity and deprivation. We have embraced righteousness rather than life and followed others' views rather than trusting our own. We have been distracted by a desire for material things, sought the approval of others and neglected a voice deep within us, the voice of the Spirit.

60. FIFTH POINT

There is a cry of wonder as I remember the people who have privileged me with their presence, who have supported and sustained me by their energy and compassion.

So many messages (almost angel-like) have come to me in a variety of ways, people, thoughts, inclinations that have warned me so that I might live. Members of my family have given me life by showing their favor and intercession.

All creation - the plants, the birds and animals, the land and sea, have all served me. What omnipresent and subtle gifts of God! Instead of swallowing me, they actually nourished, fed and as if in some miraculous way, appreciated me. This is a meditation that fills me with awe.

61. COLLOQUY

Conclude this exercise taking note of the mercy of God and the receptivity of creation. Express your thoughts about things remembered from the past and graces received most recently. This enormous gift that you reflected on during this meditation is still happening right now. God gives you creation and new life then fills you with grace to live it.

Close with an Our Father.

62. THIRD EXERCISE AND
TRIPLE COLLOQUY

Ignatius suggests that we summarize the insights from the previous meditations, that we see their value and let them take root in our hearts. Let them be anchored within us, so we will have specific reminders of the graces of God when we may need them.

In this third exercise, after the particular prayer of awareness, composing the place for prayer and considering the special grace that you are asking for this day, review the points of the previous meditation. Select those notions that have given greater consolation or the ones that have caused desolation. In some way these experiences in meditation have called you to something deeper, and in this so-called "repetition" you may find out what this call is. In closing the meditation, after having focused on a few areas that were most significant, Ignatius now presents a unique colloquy.

63. FIRST COLLOQUY

This is with Mary. I am to ask for a special grace that she might obtain three favors for me from her Son. The first is a deeper knowledge of any greed, ignorance, or resentments in my life and a knowledge of their effects.

The second favor is an understanding of the disorder in some of my actions. By tracing the cause of my actions I can discover the occasions that bring about confusion and disordered actions and the condition under which I am not my best self. Maybe I can uncover the deceptions that do not lead to satisfying results.

The third favor is to ask Mary to obtain the grace of seeing clearly the things of the world and the world's disease. I pray that I will not be fooled by pride, power, or wealth, and that I will not be bribed by praise and success, but that I will be able to see all these things as creations of God. I ask that I may realize the secret to joy and understand what inspires this joy. Close with the Hail Mary.

SECOND COLLOQUY. I will ask the same three petitions to Jesus directly, that He may obtain these graces for me from the Father. Close this colloquy with the Anima Christi prayer.

Soul of Christ, sanctify me
Body of Christ, save me
Blood of Christ, inebriate me
Water from the side of Christ, wash me
Passion of Christ, strengthen me
O good Jesus, hear me
Within thy wounds, hide me
Permit me not to be separated from thee
From the wicked foe, defend me
At the hour of my death, call me

And bid me come to thee
That with thy saints I may praise thee
For ever and ever. Amen.

THIRD COLLOQUY. I make the same request, this time directing my prayer to the Father, that the eternally present God might grant this awareness to me. Then I will close with an Our Father.

64. FOURTH EXERCISE

This exercise is a summary of the Third Exercise given above. Ignatius calls it a summary because without any additional matter or without any digression the retreatant thinks over and recalls the matter previously contemplated. In this exercise therefore, recall the matter contemplated in the previous meditation and use the three colloquies to Mary, to Jesus and the Father.

This differs from a Repetition where only those points that had given consolation or desolation are selected.

65. FIFTH EXERCISE

Begin with the preparatory prayer, the composition of place and the selected grace. Then there are five points to consider. Each one focuses on one of the five senses.

FIRST PRELUDE. In this representation of place use your five senses to imagine, enhance and relive what life must be like for certain unfortunate people. While it may not be your immediate context, it is a true world for many. You will be examining the length, breadth, and depth of suffering, violence, agony and pain that exist in peoples' lives in other places on this day. A recent newspaper will easily provide a vivid context.

SECOND PRELUDE. The grace we are asking for is to have compassion for the suffering that others endure. You might identify with one of the following: the lonely, the oppressed and the imprisoned, those with terminal illness, those who are separated from loved ones, or those who are refugees. While the love of God draws me by consolation to do the will of the Father and bring peace to the world, another motivation leads me to a concern for the millions who do not live in peace and who in fact live in fear and violence. These two motivations, the love of God and the plight of God's children will set me on fire. This is the grace we ask for in this meditation.

66. FIRST POINT

Review and reflect on current events and picture the actual situation of people living in hunger or drought today. Witness the distended bodies, bulging eyes, the lethargy, the passivity, and the utter helplessness of those who are dehydrated.

Picture the fearful who are huddled and ready to be taken prisoner to an unknown location where solace is unavailable. See one of the adolescent poor being conscripted, dragged away by militant people. It might be good to specify a particular location where war and injustice rage: Central America, Lebanon, or Israeli-controlled Palestine, the refugee camps in Southeast Asia, or the disgraceful ethnic cleansing in Eastern Europe and Africa. Picture those who are abandoned, pleading that God or man would grant sanctuary or at least send food and water. Other fears that border on trepidation can occur with city people who fear leaving their apartments day or night. Spend some time in your imagination with one of these frames of suffering humanity. It is so easy to label sin but so difficult to uproot it.

67. SECOND POINT

Hear the cries of the poor, the anger, the words of despair, the absence of joy; hear children cry. Surrounding yourself with this wailing and audible heartbreak lets you hear the results of human injustice and greed. It is painful to hear the sounds of sin.

68. THIRD POINT

Smell the dryness of the refugees' camp. How unclean! No trace or scent of vegetation - for it has been burned by man and scorched by nature. There is no sense of space, privacy or dignity because people are confined by wire and guards. What a despicable scene for God's children! The smells of cramped living conditions make even breathing a nauseous experience. What a contrast to ponder the plentiful marvels that God has given - forests and oceans, lakes and mountains! Yet because of man's inhumanity, prejudice and greed, millions of people are restricted to reservations and hovels. This is certainly not God's will or God's doing! Corruption causes a horrendous odor; the scent is death, despair and dread that can be smelled for miles and for years. The smell of sin is unbearable.

69. FOURTH POINT

Somehow taste the dryness, the bitterness and the sadness. Taste the emptiness, the disgust and the despair that screams helplessness. Is no one able to help? Will no one offer a cup of water? This drought has been going on for decades in certain areas of the world. Simply no end, no rescue, no respite! It is hard to swallow when one is close to the destitute, but to be a part of it is far worse.

70. FIFTH POINT

Ponder the sense of touch. As they pass by carrying their crosses, your presence brings hope. These are the ones that Jesus died for; His grace fills their pores. They bring vivid redemption by their slightest sunburned touch. This is where God is. It is hell on earth, yet the Lord is so profoundly present you can touch God in touching the least of these brothers and sisters. You cannot endure this passion and brutality for very long whether you are physically present to it or only imagining it.

71. COLLOQUY

Enter into conversation with Jesus, our refuge and hope, our friend and companion. We are His followers and heirs. Before Christ came into the world there were people in great need looking forward to a savior. Would someone save them by water, spirit, or blood? Jesus did it by His presence and actions. And now it is given to us to redeem others and in so doing to save ourselves, not by taking up the sword of justice and violence, but by giving what Jesus gave - life in exchange for life. And so the beauty of Christ's redemption for the world has now been passed on. We are called to be part of salvation. Even as we feel the despair and the inhumanity, we have grace, the humanity of Christ and the merciful love of God. We are not alone and they are not alone. We can form small communities of peace with confidence and patience. We are ready by God's grace.

Close with an Our Father.

OTHER EXERCISES. Other valuable topics for reflection

include inherited family or cultural biases, unchallenged theological theories, and misconceptions regarding religious practices. To analyze and modify these conditionings early into the retreat can be personally maturing and enhance the effects of the retreat experience. It will prove profitable for certain retreatants to reflect more in depth on the mystery and reality of death, judgment, and the social consequences of sin.

The first topic for reflection could be on the ultimate notion of death. It is helpful to see our life as a cycle, with God as the creator and center, and to see our origin and destination as life in God. Our life on earth is to discover and enjoy creation; our destiny is to have a fully conscious life with God. The beginning is God, the end is God and in the middle, now, God is equally present with us.

While it is difficult to be intimate with mystery, the closest experience is to live without fear. Recalling that God is life can give us a sense of oneness with time and nature and diminish any fear of death. We can appreciate the fullness of life when we see God in all things. We will be less impressed with powerful people and intimidating doctrines, and more impressed with life: its unfolding mystery and our particular vocation.

The second meditation presented here concerns the consequences of sin. By understanding the destructive intentions which eventuate in suffering we can see the logical connection between the results of sin and the preceding ignorance. The continuation of resentments and so-called swift justice cause unending damage to individuals and nations. We have the power by our behavior and attitude to continue the destruction by fostering inequality and injustice. If we expect God to punish others or to punish us, we are projecting our revengeful expectations onto God and passing these revengeful notions onto ourselves. If we justify violence by saying it is the justice of God in our own life or in the lives of others, we become devoid of human sensitivity. This is how we block out the inspiration and the grace we have today to be Christlike.

The third topic is one of judgment. Spend some time on what judgment is and where it came from. What is the consequence of judgment and how does it lead to sin and to death? Acceptance, its opposite, leads to peace and life. The message of Jesus was to give acceptance to all God's people. Since we are made in the image and likeness of God, we are therefore sons and daughters of God with full inheritance to this kingdom of acceptance. If we could ever treat each other with that understanding, or if each nationality or religion could be tolerant of others, what a kingdom of God we would have on earth!

There may arise other topics in dialogue with the Director that would be pertinent besides the three examples provided above.

72. NOTE

In the traditional thirty day retreat Ignatius recommends five meditations a day. The first one would be upon rising or before breakfast, one would be in the morning or after breakfast, the third around midday, another before dinner, and finally before sleeping.

He actually assigns the first of the exercises at midnight. To help the retreatant stay involved in the retreat around the clock is really the purpose of this intensive pattern of prayer.

To pray this often and to be enthused about each exercise is impossible outside of retreat time. While this process is unusual, it is a delightful opportunity for discovery as the retreatant pulls back the covers on the illusions and wiles that had controlled his life heretofore. Coming to the truth whether in one-self psychologically or in the world scientifically is exciting and challenging.

Assuming there is daily Mass on retreat, Ignatius mentions that a meditation before and after the Eucharist would be another way to schedule your exercises. The times that are conducive for prayer depend on the retreatant and the local opportunities. Less than five exercises is often recommended. If people have difficulty with formality or if they find that the structure is ineffective or overbearing, three meditations a day might be more than adequate. As you recall, some exercises are summaries and repetitions and their value will vary according to the person. The procedure and actual input of time and energy will depend on the health, emotional constitution and the basic disposition of the individual.

73. ADDITIONAL DIRECTIONS

Ignatius gives these directions to help you progress through the exercises better and find more readily what you desire.

PRAYER HELPS. Prior to retiring and at the conclusion of a prayer period, Ignatius suggests that you make a transition between this time and the next prayer time by asking some questions. At what hour will I be praying next? What do I want from the Lord and what are some specific points that I will include at that time. We think like this frequently and automatically in other concerns. We know when our next appointment is, where we are supposed to be and the purpose of that particular engagement. That brief reflection (for the space of a Hail Mary) tides me over and I can rest or go about my business with confidence. However, it would not be good to go beyond the subject matter of the next meditation.

74. PRAYER THOUGHTS

In coming to the prayer period there are some immediate preparations to direct your thoughts to the theme of the prayer. Before you enter into the prayer itself, look forward to the experience by becoming aware of what you will be thinking about, whom you will be meeting and what you may be doing. This will give you some sense of process and personal meaning. If you were visiting a close friend, you would be aware of the time and the place, the things you might do together, the actual greeting and welcome. You might have a request, wish to bring a present, or choose some appropriate gesture. In other words you prepare your heart for a close encounter.

If you were going to visit a friend who was a political prisoner, once again you would have different expectations. You would wonder what you could bring that would be welcome and permissible. You might reflect, "there but for the grace of God, go I." You might find yourself being aware of the presence of God and realize that you may be a sacrament of caring.

This particular mood will assist you in setting a tone for your prayer as you direct your heart and mind toward the subject of the meditation. You may be distracted by many things; that is natural. You may use whatever you can to decisively focus your attention.

75. MOMENTS OF PRAYER

As you begin your meditation, take a few moments, about the time it takes to say an Our Father, to realize that you are the center of God's love and the center is in you.

Second, sense your creativeness, be aware that you are constantly being renewed, that God is creating you and everything around you: matter, time, spirit and space.

Third, be aware of your oneness and intimacy with the world: nature life, human life, spirit life. It is the ever-present, typical experience of seeing and loving.

Fourth, sense for a moment that God is present and filling your whole being and the world around you with silence, noises, shapes, colors and motions.

Fifth, accept your createdness. You are okay right where you are at this very minute. You always were okay and always will be. You will never become more okay or less okay. You are God's design just as you are. You are the apple of His eye, His special prince or princess.

And so this brief reflection on being centered, one, created, loved, surrounded and filled with God, gives you a very gentle and yet true sense of grace as you begin this time of prayer. These initial actions can be brief, or a whole prayer period might be spent dwelling on this simple orientation.

A valuable suggestion for the retreatant is, pray before you start to pray, reflect before you begin your reflection, develop the practice of awareness before you are fully aware.

76. YOU AND YOUR GRACE

What is your treasure? Where is your heart? Seek what you desire! How selfish to seek what you wish! What will people think? What do you think? What a risk you are taking in these exercises!

Ignatius calls knowing what you desire and having the courage to seek it, Grace. You have this daily grace to see things clearly and to ask for what you desire.

In our thoughts and in the works that we do, if we stay in tune with inspirations from within, we will keep in touch with grace. As we feel a distaste or lack of interest, we trust ourselves enough to make a change.

Stay with that which inspires you until you are satisfied. Remain with the grace and do not go beyond it, as a free child who plays with a toy until satisfied, then loses interest and finds some other attractive object.

The short-lived nature of desire is discovered when we lose interest in something we desired passionately. How sensitive, how healthy, how normal! If we are open we are not disturbed when we receive a new call or intuit a new direction. Be gentle and sensitive to the ups and downs, hungers and satisfactions, lightness and darkness, exciting moments and times of quiet as we find grace in all things.

77. THE FRUIT OF PRAYER

Ignatius wants the retreatant to be aware if any discovery was made, any newness, any life. At the conclusion of this prayer exercise, reflect, "How did it go? What did I learn? Was it refreshing? Was this meaningful? Was this life-giving? Was this restful? What was the Lord like? These are questions only you can answer.

Often we get into the rut of non-reflection (non-growth). We go through the motions of prayer, but the fire is gone. The mechanism is on, the wheel is spinning, it may appear as though I am praying but the ritual is without joy. So the preceding questions can be stimulating for discovering the fruit of prayer.

78. THE IMPORTANCE OF EXTERNALS

The atmosphere of the place, the subjects I read, and the thoughts I entertain can be conducive or distracting. If I am reflecting on freedom for example, it is important that I am free before and during meditation and that I sense this freedom as much as possible throughout the day. How free was Jesus to go to Jerusalem, to visit his friends, to go to the homes of pharisees or publicans? What kind of atmosphere would you set up if you were to meditate on freedom? Think of yourself in an ideal situation where freedom is realized and enjoyed.

If I am meditating on Christ present with the poor, it will be helpful to read articles about the poor or to walk through or visit a poor neighborhood. In this way, life leads me to pray and my prayer helps me to see life in a new way.

79. MAKING THE MOST OF PRAYER

Past patterns will always have the strongest influence on the style of my prayer, so it is important to observe attentively and think creatively to instill variety. Sometimes the topic of the meditation is somber and serious and I will naturally find myself preferring simpler meals, quieter places and more solitude. I may find myself withdrawing from typical attractions and the company of others. On the other hand if I am meditating on something joyful I will utilize joyful things like the light of day, the stars at night and the uplifting spirits of others, the laughter of children to blend into my day and prayer. I may notice that I will spend my free time observing people and watching my reactions to them.

The milieu for prayer should be as beneficial as the acoustics and atmosphere of a theater would be for a live performance. It would be worthwhile in each particular meditation to engage your imagination as you plan and create a personal setting.

80. MY IDEAS AND IMPRESSIONS

The words that I use during the day will influence my spiritual exercises since they will express where my thoughts and intentions have been. If I could record the words spoken this day, how would I characterize them? What proportion would be friendly, welcoming, inviting, impersonal, critical, interfering, fearful or insecure? What characterized my silent times? Were they actually filled with many words, just unspoken?

81. OBSERVATIONS

What I look at will have a direct connection with my thoughts and feelings during and at the times surrounding my prayer time.

PENANCE

82. POSITIVE AND NEGATIVE FORMS

Soberly reflecting on one's actions is a form of interior penance that stimulates growth. Trial and error, the so-called "Scientific Method" provides progress through experiment and mistakes. The best way to teach is to allow people to learn for themselves. The best way to learn is to experience for yourself.

There are some penances that do not facilitate growth, but actually disturb the human spirit.

Many people think that if something is a law, it is sacred and takes on a charism that is holier than the individual. When we have been told that we have violated some commandment there ensues a feeling of guilt, a sense of threat.

We might question the extent of our iniquity and wonder what punishment will follow. Besides remorse and an admission of the wrongdoing, a firm purpose of amendment is recommended as well as a penance. As creatures of habit, we become accustomed to penance and punishment, and while it is cruel, the deprivation and practice continue.

Restrictions and restraints from authority figures are forms of exterior penance. When a political prisoner is confined for what he believes, he is deprived of normal God-given freedoms because he does not conform to authority. It is actually a form of revenge that is unforgiving and spiritless. It is not justice. We are capable of doing this to ourselves when we act scrupulously or in a rigid way. We can actually punish ourselves for not submitting to a set of ideas.

When can Penance be a value? And what is the value of penance? A shower in the morning and cool water on the face: is that a penance or a blessing? To avoid ambiguity, an appropriate word or synonym for penance would be "stimulation". There are internal and external ways of waking up, of igniting and giving vitality to life. Stimulation moves people to a new level; it shakes them out of their past, their dreams and their fantasies. Stimulation is the catalyst for clarity. It can be soothing and gentle, or it can be surprising and tingling. But it is not helpful when harm in any form occurs. Destructive results negate the positive meaning of penance and replace it with abuse and abhorrence.

83. CHOOSING PENANCES

The first kind of exterior penance concerns eating. What is the best program for this person at this time?

If you were to plan a healthy menu for a child what would you select, and how would you go about it? As an aware parent, you would have a comprehensive knowledge of the child's reactions to food and of basic nutrition. If the director and retreatant are equally sensitive to nutrition, these decisions will be simple. If the director knows the retreatant, his personality and preferences, suggestions will be well received.

To wake a child from a sound sleep would normally be disturbing but the adult who understands the child and knows what is truly in his best interest will be tolerant in dealing with the reactions and most sensitive in explaining the reasons.

When you are teaching someone that the knife is sharp, the stove is hot, or the traffic is dangerous, you are not intending to teach fear and anxiety, or to embarrass him by exposing his ignorance and inferiority. Because you want him to understand and pay attention you might use some dramatic or special effects. The words and emphasis you use and the stimulating way you describe the message are critical.

Penances can have value if they are treated not as goods in themselves but simply as arbitrary personal rules that only derive meaning from their fruitfulness. The purpose of penances in Ignatius' era was not always one of stimulation and awareness. Today the choice of penances must be the retreatant's personal decision, for the goal is to give vitality to his life.

84. THE TRUE MEANING

Ignatius says, "It is not penance when we do away with the superfluous..." One rule of penance is that nothing should be imposed or inflicted that would cause pain, sickness, or disease. Another is that penances are to be consoling and are meant to bring about consolation. In other words the good end to be attained must involve a good means as well. We should not be fooled by the types, rituals or traditions of penance. Three things to avoid in choosing penances are: any actions that would be considered extreme, any feelings of superiority, and any behavior that is not open to question.

A person who is fasting before a race experiences a joy in the fasting and in the training. If there is discomfort before, the particular practice should be re-evaluated, for the ailment could continue and the person would not be at his best physically, mentally, or emotionally. This would counteract any visible gain. There is no guarantee that a penance is good except by the evaluation, analysis and decision of the individual. Is it good and enjoyable for me now? This is the most honest question and one easily verifiable.

Ignatius does not want anyone to be caught up in worldly pride; it would be counterproductive and deceitful. Yet the tendency for approval and approbation is in every community and strata of society. Pride is ugly and unsatisfying; words of praise are as fleeting as the sounds they make. Phrases like "I am better than I was, or I am better than others," create false highs and are self-defeating.

Any condemnation of the past or acclamation of the self is divisive and amplifies our desperate need for acceptance. We victimize ourselves by our own standards. What a waste!

The presumption that I am doing a penance or fasting so that God will answer my prayers is fatuous. Such reasoning insinuates that a formula can control God's will, or worse, that God will only help us if we beg and abuse ourselves. In such a state I would be manipulating myself in God's name and building up resentments toward this image of God that I have created. Hopefully, just listening to such an approach would be an overt reminder of my crooked and programmed intentions.

Another rule of penance is to avoid the tendency to follow the penance of others. How easily we are moved by fame, founders, writers and authority figures! What a mockery this would be in face of the precious and unique giftedness, spirit, and inspiration that we possess. Only our awake, sensitive, and personal choice can be clearly effective. "Come to a happy mean," Ignatius writes.

Another designation for the term penance is diet. It may not have been used in Ignatius' day, but people trying to attain their desired weight and to regulate their health will try certain things until they find the ones that work for them. People who are unhappy because they are lethargic or lazy will want to do something to change, especially if it proves to be less painful than the present passivity.

Ignatius provides different approaches regarding food, diet, and amount of sleep. The technique includes a special awareness of self, as well as related persons, places and things. The method is to discover which is unnecessary and superfluous. Find the things in your life that are dragging your spirit, and as you truthfully discover how to buoy up your spirit, you will be happier and feel better. So the notion of penance as stimulation will make the search and evaluation easier. You will notice that the effects are sensible and practical.

When you locate the area causing a disturbance or anxiety, there is immediate relief. If there is a healthy response, you feel a strong desire to make some corrections. There is joy in the discovery as well as in the prescription. When you discover what you are allergic to there is an incomparable feeling of freedom and elation. It gives clear direction to your life.

Penances have nothing to do with pain, pride or punishment, neither should they be religious, sacrificial or sanctimonious. While this clarification might be helpful, there is still a difficulty to be encountered, which is the rut, the deep seated behavior caused by habit. Physical or psychological tendencies have formed repetitive unreflective behavior.

85. KNOWING YOUR LIMITS

Ignatius writes of feeling some pain during penance akin to that experienced by an athlete doing stretching exercises. We also stretch, test and reach our limits on various days performing different tasks in various situations. We are capable of feeling hunger and fatigue. Some aches and stiffness remind us that we have strained some muscle. How healthy a response! Unless medically prohibited we feel no doubt or fear in these circumstances. Even after surgery one needs to exercise for circulation and adaptation. So too with our spiritual life! There will be some discomfort as one changes from a rather sedentary existence to one of engagement and activity. As one turns off the television, forgoes busy activities and distractions, he will be able to spend more courageous time in exchanging ideas and feelings with others. This intimate behavior is more satisfying and more nourishing for the human spirit.

When important areas of our life have lain dormant, professional therapy is often required to estimate the extent of the damage and to propose an appropriate program for growth.

86. SENSIBLE APPROACHES

Any approach that is not clearly chosen and visibly life-giving must be questioned by the use of common sense and reason. Pain instilled for the sake of pain or for the sake of manipulation is destructive. There are many people who used authority to impose sacrifices on others. It is the history of the world and the nature of society's institutions. Beware!

Is novacaine your preference? Fine! Is the ordeal of allergy testing more discomforting than the allergic reaction? Your decision! Freedom and choice must be preserved so that we do not compromise our integrity to conform to some convention or for the fleeting approval of others.

Talk to your spiritual director if there is any painful experience. Even rising at an earlier hour than usual should be discussed with one's director to check the pros, cons, values and consequences. An honest examination will reveal if any of the following are present: pride, past programming, imitation of an ideal, or unrealistic expectations. Simply, is it or is it not good for you? Is it sensibly consoling or does it create strain or anxiety? Whether you refer to it as penance or stimulation, share it with the director.

To do calisthenics is helpful if one is about to stretch one's muscles in a particular venture. To do it simply for the sake of exercise is appealing to a very limited number of people. However, joining with friends, adding music, donning a comfortable outfit, and changing the name to aerobics makes it a popular activity. When sensations or movements of the body are combined with other levels of stimulation people look forward to it. Afterwards, there is a feeling of satisfaction and delight, rather than relief. In fact the effects of the stimulation continue to give life. A far cry from calisthenics, sacrifice and penance!

It is great when we can do heart and emotional aerobics. This is what Retreat, Spiritual Exercises and Penances can be. This aerobic retreat can revive the apostolic spirit, resolve differences between people and bring integration, rhythm and joy.

The process of personal awareness, sharing of feelings, combined with mutual acceptance and understanding bring about the miracles of conflict resolution.

To be creative about stimulation, we must look at areas that could use some awakening. Then, without hesitation we will treat our body with the same care as we treat our spirit; and we will treat our spirit as God does, without interference, with freedom and sensitivity. This is what Ignatius means by "sensible".

87. EFFICACIOUS PENANCES

Ignatius writes that the principal reason for exterior penance is to secure good effects. It is healthy to see what the intentions for seeking stimulation are. What have been the effects, how realistic are the expectations, and is the stimulation appropriate for the desired result? Are there better ways of achieving these results? If we notice that a certain modus operandi is no longer productive, we may desire a new approach. If we are not satisfied with our use of things it is the signal to take a different approach. Once we admit that what had worked before is no longer effective, we are dealing with reality, and the chances of finding a solution are optimistic. This could include anything from a slight change in diet to a radical change in behavior patterns, time schedules or reflection time. To find the key and the most direct cure might be a matter of time, may involve further reflection, or might need a different environment. A "concerted" exercise and discovery program is recommended. We must take our lives seriously. We are worth it; life is worth it.

Some of our problems may be communication difficulties, resistance to intimacy, insufficient free time or compulsive behavior. Whatever is out of harmony now may have functioned well previously. Maybe the solution will be in the area of taking the initiative: for example, inviting people to a gathering, giving your time to a social project, or possibly spending quiet time writing your thoughts. Whether the concern is community, family, work, personal or apostolic, the secret is creating time for reflection and stirring up some life to "make waves."

One of the purposes of penance is to help people who are unawake or insensitive.

People are disillusioned and drugged either deliberately or accidentally. Defenses that are supposed to help people survive also prevent them from deep and joyful experiences. Whenever we discover insensitivity, there are careful ways of probing for signs of life. For example, those who have lived and seen only the luxurious side of life without having spent time with the rest of the world have wealthy defenses which would make them fragile and incapable of experiencing real life outside their walls. Even their pain has been artificial. They need to be careful not to expose themselves too drastically to the unexpected dismay, disgust, confusion, and even guilt when they realize that eighty percent of the world has supported the twenty percent in their luxury. And worse, the myth is that the wealthy are supporting the destitute!

For the insensitive, like the indoctrinated and drugged, nothing will change while they are living an illusion. They see certain people as enemies, others as lazy, others as deserving of whatever befalls them. They cannot see Christ except in magnificent buildings and marble statues, in ancient rituals and ceremonial robes.

The sensitive, the aware, are heartbroken when they see God's people, their own brothers and sisters suffer at the hands of a greed-infested economic system still called "the trickle down effect". But similar ones have been in effect everywhere that pride and power are unbridled.

What is the proper stimulus? We do not need to wake up the vast spectrum of caring individuals. There are thousands of Catholic Relief workers, Maryknoll missionaries, Jesuit Refugee servers and Peace Corps volunteers who believe the good news and are living it. But we have observed firsthand that man's ideologies and policies still destroy, violate and ravage nation after nation. To realize that people support their government's investment in atrocities wakes us up to see what the enemy of God's people looks like. We are only imprisoned by our own illusions.

To see firsthand the fear that surrounds people and from which there is no exit touches the heart. Fortunately, two graces accompany such a sacred presence: the courage to cope and the strength to contribute. This type of radical penance is a graced life for the volunteers as well as the victims. The huddled, oppressed masses of poor are caught in the crossfire of conflicting ideologies. Those dedicated to alleviating their burdens are the true disciples of Jesus. Other disciples are those who write, vote, lobby and protest for peace. Then there are the soup kitchens and those who donate food, clothes, and money. What is most stimulating for your heart? How do you work for peace? What gives you a strong sense that you are part of the cure?

While a typical reason for penance is to attain something, some teachers emphasized penance as necessary for forgiveness. This was reinforced by implying that confessing and then performing a penance was a condition of forgiveness. This contradicts the belief that God is the eternal and loving forgiver. It is important to clarify this lest any ritual undermines one's trust in God. This misunderstanding could distract people once again from enjoying the beauty of God's love and the freedom of unconditional forgiveness.

There is a difference between law and love. It is essential for our mental health that we remember that God is forgiveness. In the Christian faith we believe that Christ announced by His life, death and resurrection that we are one with God. We always were united with God, pre-life, in life and after life. Jesus did not judge, accuse, or hold men's sins against them. To motivate people to do penance by promising forgiveness of their sins or the forgiveness of God would be misleading and may emphasize conditional love.

It is customary to accept rules as right and good when they emanate from right minded people seeking the common good. Rules are prejudiced and harmful when they are the composition of a select committee who do not truly represent the will of the people, but are rather an imposition of the committee's will on the people.

How do we find reasonable and personal motives for waking people up to attain the fullness of freedom they hunger for?

The healthy answer is to turn to the Lord, asking Jesus, "What would You do in this situation?" True penance is a metanoia, putting on the mind of Christ. We will assuredly come to the truth, for Christ wants us to be free. Being true to ourselves is our best chance.

88. HUMILITY

Once we break away free from one illusion we then need to foster the new truth that we realize. When we understand how oppressive a particular pattern was, and once we free ourselves from performing it, we still need to fill that void with positive behavior. Ignatius says to do it privately without show, without pride.

89. BE YOUR OWN MASTER

With penance or discipline (rules that work for me) it is important that I am not playing parent/child games or religious/spiritual ones with my life. If I think that God is pleased when I eat vegetables or skip dessert, that my sacrifices please God, that resting less, working more, or going to church is making God happier or winning God's favor, I have been sorely misled. It is either a belief based on superstition or a childhood tale that has never been examined or understood.

How do you get another person to do what you want him to do? Why would you want to subjugate another in the first place? To have mastery over another is to deny the presence of Christ and presents serious obstacles to finding God in the other. How do you motivate yourself to do something you do not want to do? Why would you want to? "Let no one be your master." It is the direct opposite of charity, freedom and happiness. To submit to another "in the name of God" is tantamount to asking God to bless slavery. To do this to yourself is equally abominable though more common. This use of godly words is seductive and confusing because these apparently religious motives make the journey to true spiritual freedom more complex.

Doctors say, listen to your body; retreat directors say, listen to your heart. Whom do you listen to? Who is the authority that typically dictates to you? Did you ever relinquish your mind and will? If so, when did you get it back? How did this authority acquire such power over you, and how did you finally escape? "Do not allow yourselves to be slaves again." (Galatians 5: 1)

90. THE GRACE OF PENANCE

When a penance becomes a distraction and takes up too much time, thought or energy, it ceases to be helpful. Sometimes the most effective penance is one that provides a pinch of flavoring, a twist, a shake or a brief exchange. In this process do not be anxious, jealous or possessive. The grace of others would never work for us; we each have our own unique grace.

The reason why we behaved in certain ways in the past was due to the degree of grace and wisdom we had. So do not compare or judge the past too harshly.

The things we want to do as well as those we are capable of doing are parts of our unique journey. Grace is the ability, desire and courage that is strictly ours. Grace is taking into consideration God's gift to be precisely who we are at this moment.

Grace and Consolation go hand in hand. God knows and loves Himself. As we get to know and love ourselves, we become like God.

THE KINGDOM OF CHRIST

91. THE CALL OF AN EARTHLY LEADER

The opening prayer is one of awareness. The tone is set by a sense of our oneness and presence with God.

FIRST PRELUDE. Let us picture a village of poor inhabitants, in a situation that prevents the people from bettering their plight. The powerless are the most neglected because of ignorance, prejudiced beliefs, skin color, and accidental time and place of their birth. Some combination of the above has caused their confinement, apartheid or refugee status. See the society around them that fostered their imprisonment and corralled them as animals without freedom to move or to own land and with no chance for growth. Picture a scene similar to this, for Jesus is tangibly present with the poor.

SECOND PRELUDE. Ask to hear the call of Christ, so that you may discover what grace will fill you with inspiration and happiness. Pray that you will be led by goodness and consolation in all your actions. To know what grace moves your heart is a very healthy form of selfishness. For in this meditation you are asking that you can find your own joy in life with people who are your contemporaries.

FIRST PART

92. FIRST POINT

Picture a President or renowned leader of a country who also is inspired, has a full and generous heart, and does not cling to wealth, prestige and power. Hear his words, listen to his plan of helping the poor by offering his services and his life to aid the outcasts of society. He plans to become one with them so that they will believe that they have an identical inheritance. This might assure them that they really are loved and are truly God's unforgotten people. This renowned leader will be with them day and night; he will work with them, eat with them, study with them during the day, and share their roof or whatever shelter they possess at night.

93. SECOND POINT

This President then confronts you, would you be willing to "share in the toil with me" and to share in the consequences, the satisfaction as well as the hardship? You will be working side by side with this prince of a person. You will be asked to do no more than he is doing, but maybe as much. This is a truly unusual person; this is nobility; this is generosity. This is the work of the kingdom. But is the offer practical? Are there any chances for success? Why dream of such service?

It seems unusual to even fantasize that a government leader with wealth and power would even remotely ponder such a gift of life. It would be more difficult to picture a Pope or a President who would stoop this far. Yet it is not beyond our imagination, it has happened in our time, with the poorest of the poor. It happened in India with Gandhi; it happened in the United States with King; it happened in El Salvador with Romero; and it occurs every time a person gives his life a day at a time for others. It is happening every day.

94. THIRD POINT

Okay, it is time for an answer. Listen as if the situation were real, the invitation were real; and be aware of the nature of your reaction. Meditate for a while on this invitation and grace, and listen to your heart. Where are you called, where are you chosen, where will you find your greatest joy in this life?

95. THE CALL OF CHRIST THE KING

Most governments and religions desire obedience from their followers and recognition from their neighbors, and too frequently they crave self-aggrandizement and self-preservation. On occasion they resort to mandates or ultimatums in the name of defense, progress, or even justice. Often these principles are professed as an excuse to enforce their rules or their will on others, sometimes resorting to physical or emotional cruelty. Under the guise of the common good, reputedly civilized governments have chosen violence to attain their ends. Some have violated the commandment not to kill by ordering the deaths of their own people in the name of justice. Of course there is a long history to capital punishment - Churches of the past tried to threaten people with eternal damnation and excommunication when they refused to follow their mandates. Physical as well as mental tortures have been implemented to attain the ends of these institutions. They have blasphemed the ideals they were appointed to represent - tolerance, equality, compassion and charity.

So Ignatius is talking about a king and a kingdom not espousing this world's style of justice. He is speaking of an earthly prince who represents a kingdom of mercy and compassion, of love and of peace, who never leads by threats of violence and domination.

SECOND PART

FIRST POINT. Ignatius wants us to hear the invitation of the Eternal King who is willing to give His life for peace, not by taking up the sword against others, but by laying down His own life. He is a true leader, a genuine shepherd, an inspiring person with a challenging invitation. Is it appealing, or does it seem impractical and unreal? Jesus invites us, "Join me in this enterprise if you are willing to labor with Me." According to your ability and grace, do you find it appealing to help others find this peace and liberation? You must desire to bring about a true community where there is wholehearted sharing of possessions, ideas and feelings.

96. SECOND POINT
There is an incomparable joy when one alleviates the burdens people carry. This is a refreshing invitation for those who have the ability to reason and the freedom to make decisions. It is attractive to those who have reflected on the goods of this world and who have weighed the consequences of becoming attached to them. Persons who think they are still deprived cannot see the beauty of this appeal of Christ. That is understandable! But for those who have tasted the goodness of the world and enjoyed the privilege of serving humanity, there is no deeper release or greater human satisfaction. What an honor it is to give the assurance of forgiveness, to cut the barbed wires of fear and slavery or to open the borders for excluded races, colors and creeds!

What indescribable joy it is to see the oneness of mankind, to be part of it, to help cause it, to be another Christ!

97. THIRD POINT
For those who wish to give a greater proof of their love and to distinguish themselves in the service of the King, they will not only offer themselves entirely for the work when the occasion arises, but they will find themselves looking for opportunities to serve. They will find great satisfaction in making a special offering to the King, by Christ's favor and help.

I pray that I might be able to imitate Jesus in bearing rejection, abuse, and poverty, both actual and spiritual, that I may have the grace of being able to turn the other cheek as Jesus did, without the slightest trace of resentment or revenge, jealousy or regret, that I may be inspired by the beauty of this unconditional Lover. As I see the value of this state of life, I ask that I may be filled with assurance to adopt it in working for peace.

98. ETERNAL LORD OF ALL THINGS.

Ignatius wrote a personal prayer at this stage of his retreat experience. He addressed it to The Eternal Lord. It would be preferable if you would write your own prayer of dedication, your own personal offering as you profess your desire to serve and imitate Christ.

Eternal Lord of all things, in the presence of Thy infinite goodness, and of Thy glorious mother, and of all the saints of Thy heavenly court, this is the offering of myself which I make with Thy favor and help. I protest that it is my earnest desire and my deliberate choice, provided only it is for Thy greater service and praise, to imitate Thee in bearing all wrongs and all abuse and all poverty, both actual and spiritual, should Thy most holy majesty deign to choose and admit me to such a state and way of life.

99. NOTE I

This exercise on the call of Christ should be performed at least twice.

100. NOTE II

During the Second Week and thereafter, it will be very profitable to read some passages from the Following of Christ, from the Gospels and from the Lives of the Saints.

For the Introduction and First Week of the Exercises, Ignatius in his wisdom did not prescribe any particular scripture passages. The stories written about Jesus and the simply awesome life that He led require guidance and preparation to apply the myths, miracles and meaning into one's own life.

There are really two scriptures in life. The most obvious is the ancient writings themselves, filled with references by and about the holy founder of each early religion. Each religion cherishes her traditional fragments, scrolls and her historical translations.

The second scripture in life is the script that each one is living individually. Each one of us from day one is God's very own creation with a family of origin, a continuous salvation history, a unique personal call and a Spirit leading us as vividly as the Spirit's movement in any other time in history.

Of course our daily lived scripture is not written down fully, neither was the life of Jesus, or Moses or Abraham. But it is scripture; it is God writing in us and all around us with all its power and promise.

Ignatius starts the retreatant out with observations of reality, reflections on the spirit working in the retreatant's life to the present day, with practical and philosophical questions like, what have I done with my life so far and how does this measure up with my best intentions, hopes and inspirations?

Most retreatants today (over 450 years after the original writing of The Exercises) have sufficient background to combine the initial Exercises with pertinent Scripture texts. And so the following scripture passages from the Old and New Testament are included for the Introduction and First Week.

SCRIPTURE TEXTS FOR THE INTRODUCTION AND FIRST WEEK

GENESIS 1:14 - 18

GOD SAID, "LET THERE BE LIGHTS IN THE VAULT OF HEAVEN TO DIVIDE DAY FROM NIGHT, AND LET THEM INDICATE FESTIVALS, DAYS AND YEARS. LET THERE BE LIGHTS IN THE VAULT OF HEAVEN TO SHINE ON THE EARTH." AND SO IT WAS. GOD MADE THE TWO GREAT LIGHTS: THE GREATER LIGHT TO GOVERN THE DAY, THE SMALLER LIGHT TO GOVERN THE NIGHT, AND THE STARS. GOD SET THEM IN THE VAULT OF HEAVEN TO SHINE ON THE EARTH, TO GOVERN THE DAY AND THE NIGHT AND TO DIVIDE LIGHT FROM DARKNESS. GOD SAW THAT IT WAS GOOD.

GENESIS 1:26 - 28

GOD SAID, "LET US MAKE MAN IN OUR OWN IMAGE, IN THE LIKENESS OF OURSELVES, AND LET THEM BE MASTERS OF THE FISH OF THE SEA, THE BIRDS OF HEAVEN, THE CATTLE, ALL THE WILD BEASTS AND ALL THE REPTILES THAT CRAWL UPON THE EARTH." GOD CREAT-ED MAN IN THE IMAGE OF HIMSELF, IN THE IMAGE OF GOD HE CREATED HIM, MALE AND FEMALE HE CREATED THEM. GOD BLESSED THEM, SAYING TO THEM, "BE FRUITFUL, MUL-TIPLY, FILL THE EARTH AND CONQUER IT. BE MASTERS OF THE FISH OF THE SEA, THE BIRDS OF HEAVEN AND ALL LIVING ANIMALS ON THE EARTH."

DEUTERONOMY 30:19 - 20

I SET BEFORE YOU LIFE OR DEATH, BLESSING OR CURSE. CHOOSE LIFE, THEN, SO THAT YOU AND YOUR DESCENDANTS MAY LIVE, IN THE LOVE OF YAHWEH YOUR GOD, OBEYING HIS

VOICE, CLINGING TO HIM; FOR IN THIS YOUR
LIFE CONSISTS.

PSALM 91: 5 - 6, 15

YOU NEED NOT FEAR THE TERRORS OF NIGHT,
THE ARROW THAT FLIES IN THE DAYTIME, THE
PLAGUE THAT STALKS IN THE DARK, THE
SCOURGE THAT WREAKS HAVOC IN BROAD
DAYLIGHT. I ANSWER EVERYONE WHO INVOKES
ME, I AM WITH THEM WHEN THEY ARE IN TROU-
BLE; I BRING THEM SAFETY AND HONOR.

PSALM 103: 8, 13

YAHWEH IS TENDER AND COMPASSIONATE,
SLOW TO ANGER, MOST LOVING; AS TENDERLY
AS A FATHER TREATS HIS CHILDREN, SO YAH-
WEH TREATS THOSE WHO FEAR HIM.

PSALM 131: 1 - 2

YAHWEH, MY HEART HAS NO LOFTY AMBI-
TIONS, MY EYES DO NOT LOOK TOO HIGH. I AM
NOT CONCERNED WITH GREAT AFFAIRS OR
MARVELS BEYOND MY SCOPE. ENOUGH FOR ME
TO KEEP MY SOUL TRANQUIL AND QUIET LIKE A
CHILD IN ITS MOTHER'S ARMS, AS CONTENT AS
A CHILD THAT HAS BEEN WEANED.

WISDOM 3: 1 - 9

BUT THE SOULS OF THE VIRTUOUS ARE IN THE
HANDS OF GOD, NO TORMENT SHALL EVER
TOUCH THEM. IN THE EYES OF THE UNWISE,
THEY DID APPEAR TO DIE, THEIR GOING
LOOKED LIKE A DISASTER, THEIR LEAVING US,
LIKE ANNIHILATION; BUT THEY ARE IN PEACE.
IF THEY EXPERIENCED PUNISHMENT AS MEN
SEE IT, THEIR HOPE WAS RICH WITH IMMOR-
TALITY; SLIGHT WAS THEIR AFFLICTION,
GREAT WILL THEIR BLESSINGS BE. GOD HAS
PUT THEM TO THE TEST AND PROVED THEM
WORTHY TO BE WITH HIM; HE HAS TESTED
THEM LIKE GOLD IN A FURNACE, AND ACCEPT-

ED THEM AS A HOLOCAUST. WHEN THE TIME
COMES FOR HIS VISITATION THEY WILL SHINE
OUT; AS SPARKS RUN THROUGH THE STUBBLE,
SO WILL THEY. THEY SHALL JUDGE NATIONS,
RULE OVER PEOPLES, AND THE LORD WILL BE
THEIR KING FOR EVER. THEY WHO TRUST IN
HIM WILL UNDERSTAND THE TRUTH, THOSE
WHO ARE FAITHFUL WILL LIVE WITH HIM IN
LOVE; FOR GRACE AND MERCY AWAIT THOSE
HE HAS CHOSEN.

SONG OF SONGS 2: 3 - 4

AS AN APPLE TREE AMONG THE TREES OF THE
ORCHARD, SO IS MY BELOVED AMONG THE
YOUNG MEN. IN HIS LONGED-FOR SHADE I AM
SEATED AND HIS FRUIT IS SWEET TO MY
TASTE. HE HAS TAKEN ME TO HIS BANQUET
HALL, AND THE BANNER HE RAISES OVER ME
IS LOVE.

ISAIAH 9: 1 - 2

THE PEOPLE THAT WALKED IN DARKNESS
HAVE SEEN A GREAT LIGHT; ON THOSE WHO
LIVE IN A LAND OF DEEP SHADOW A LIGHT
HAS SHONE. YOU HAVE MADE THEIR GLAD-
NESS GREATER, YOU HAVE MADE THEIR JOY
INCREASE; THEY REJOICE IN YOUR PRESENCE
AS MEN REJOICE AT HARVEST TIME, AS MEN
ARE HAPPY WHEN THEY ARE DIVIDING THE
SPOILS.

ISAIAH 12: 2 - 3

SEE NOW, HE IS THE GOD OF MY SALVATION I
HAVE TRUST NOW AND NO FEAR, FOR YAHWEH
IS MY STRENGTH, MY SONG, HE IS MY SALVA-
TION. AND YOU WILL DRAW WATER JOYFULLY
FROM THE SPRINGS OF SALVATION.

ISAIAH 43: 1 - 3

BUT NOW, THUS SAYS YAHWEH, WHO CREATED
YOU, JACOB, WHO FORMED YOU, ISRAEL: DO

NOT BE AFRAID, FOR I HAVE REDEEMED YOU; I
HAVE CALLED YOU BY YOUR NAME, YOU ARE
MINE. SHOULD YOU PASS THROUGH THE SEA, I
WILL BE WITH YOU; OR THROUGH RIVERS,
THEY WILL NOT SWALLOW YOU UP. SHOULD
YOU WALK THROUGH FIRE, YOU WILL NOT BE
SCORCHED AND THE FLAMES WILL NOT BURN
YOU. FOR I AM YAHWEH, YOUR GOD, THE HOLY
ONE OF ISRAEL, YOUR SAVIOR. I GIVE EGYPT
FOR YOUR RANSOM, AND EXCHANGE CUSH
AND SEBA FOR YOU.

ISAIAH 43: 4 - 5

BECAUSE YOU ARE PRECIOUS IN MY EYES,
BECAUSE YOU ARE HONORED AND I LOVE YOU,
I GIVE MEN IN EXCHANGE FOR YOU, PEOPLES
IN RETURN FOR YOUR LIFE. DO NOT BE
AFRAID, FOR I AM WITH YOU.

ISAIAH 44: 24

THUS SAYS YAHWEH, YOUR REDEEMER, HE
WHO FORMED YOU IN THE WOMB: I, MYSELF,
YAHWEH, MADE ALL THINGS, I ALONE SPREAD
OUT THE HEAVENS. WHEN I GAVE THE EARTH
SHAPE, DID ANYONE HELP ME?

ISAIAH 48: 6 - 7

YOU HAVE HEARD AND SEEN ALL THIS, WILL
YOU NOT ADMIT IT? NOW I AM REVEALING
NEW THINGS TO YOU, THINGS HIDDEN AND
UNKNOWN TO YOU, CREATED JUST NOW, THIS
VERY MOMENT, OF THESE THINGS YOU HAVE
HEARD NOTHING UNTIL NOW, SO THAT YOU
CANNOT SAY, "OH YES, I KNEW ALL THIS."

ISAIAH 55: 2

WHY SPEND MONEY ON WHAT IS NOT BREAD,
YOUR WAGES ON WHAT FAILS TO SATISFY?
LISTEN, LISTEN TO ME, AND YOU WILL HAVE
GOOD THINGS TO EAT AND RICH FOOD TO
ENJOY.

ISAIAH 55: 3

PAY ATTENTION, COME TO ME; LISTEN, AND
YOUR SOUL WILL LIVE. WITH YOU I WILL
MAKE AN EVERLASTING COVENANT OUT OF
THE FAVORS PROMISED TO DAVID.

ISAIAH 61: 1

THE SPIRIT OF THE LORD YAHWEH HAS BEEN
GIVEN TO ME, FOR YAHWEH HAS ANOINTED
ME. HE HAS SENT ME TO BRING GOOD NEWS
TO THE POOR, TO BIND UP HEARTS THAT ARE
BROKEN; TO PROCLAIM LIBERTY TO CAPTIVES,
FREEDOM TO THOSE IN PRISON;

JEREMIAH 31: 33 - 34

THIS IS THE COVENANT I WILL MAKE WITH
THE HOUSE OF ISRAEL WHEN THOSE DAYS
ARRIVE - IT IS YAHWEH WHO SPEAKS. DEEP
WITHIN THEM I WILL PLANT MY LAW, WRITING
IT ON THEIR HEARTS. THEN I WILL BE THEIR
GOD AND THEY SHALL BE MY PEOPLE. THERE
WILL BE NO FURTHER NEED FOR NEIGHBOR TO
TRY TO TEACH NEIGHBOR OR BROTHER TO SAY
TO BROTHER, "LEARN TO KNOW YAHWEH!"
NO, THEY WILL ALL KNOW ME, THE LEAST NO
LESS THAN THE GREATEST - IT IS YAHWEH
WHO SPEAKS - SINCE I WILL FORGIVE THEIR
INIQUITY AND NEVER CALL THEIR SIN TO
MIND.

ACTS 2: 17 - 19

IN THE DAYS TO COME - IT IS THE LORD WHO
SPEAKS - I WILL POUR OUT MY SPIRIT ON ALL
MANKIND. THEIR SONS AND DAUGHTERS
SHALL PROPHESY, YOUR YOUNG MEN SHALL
SEE VISIONS, YOUR OLD MEN SHALL DREAM
DREAMS. EVEN ON MY SLAVES, MEN AND
WOMEN, IN THOSE DAYS, I WILL POUR OUT MY
SPIRIT. I WILL DISPLAY PORTENTS IN HEAVEN
ABOVE AND SIGNS ON EARTH BELOW.

ACTS 4: 29 - 31

AND NOW, LORD, TAKE NOTE OF THEIR
THREATS AND HELP YOUR SERVANTS TO PRO-
CLAIM YOUR MESSAGE WITH ALL BOLDNESS,
BY STRETCHING OUT YOUR HAND TO HEAL
AND TO WORK MIRACLES AND MARVELS
THROUGH THE NAME OF YOUR HOLY SERVANT
JESUS. AS THEY PRAYED, THE HOUSE WHERE
THEY WERE ASSEMBLED ROCKED; THEY WERE
ALL FILLED WITH THE HOLY SPIRIT AND BEGAN
TO PROCLAIM THE WORD OF GOD BOLDLY.

ROMANS 8: 15 - 16

THE SPIRIT YOU RECEIVED IS NOT THE SPIRIT
OF SLAVES BRINGING FEAR INTO YOUR LIVES
AGAIN; IT IS THE SPIRIT OF SONS, AND IT
MAKES US CRY OUT, "ABBA, FATHER!" THE
SPIRIT HIMSELF AND OUR SPIRIT BEAR UNITED
WITNESS THAT WE ARE CHILDREN OF GOD.

ROMANS 8: 35

NOTHING THEREFORE CAN COME BETWEEN US
AND THE LOVE OF CHRIST, EVEN IF WE ARE
TROUBLED OR WORRIED, OR BEING PERSECUT-
ED, OR LACKING FOOD OR CLOTHES, OR BEING
THREATENED OR EVEN ATTACKED.

ROMANS 8: 38 - 39

FOR I AM CERTAIN OF THIS: NEITHER DEATH
NOR LIFE, NO ANGEL, NO PRINCE, NOTHING
THAT EXISTS, NOTHING STILL TO COME, NOT
ANY POWER, OR HEIGHT OR DEPTH, NOR ANY
CREATED THING, CAN EVER COME BETWEEN
US AND THE LOVE OF GOD MADE VISIBLE IN
CHRIST JESUS OUR LORD.

ROMANS 14: 7 - 8

THE LIFE AND DEATH OF EACH OF US HAS ITS
INFLUENCE ON OTHERS; IF WE LIVE, WE LIVE
FOR THE LORD; AND IF WE DIE, WE DIE FOR
THE LORD, SO THAT ALIVE OR DEAD WE
BELONG TO THE LORD.

I CORINTHIANS 12: 8 - 9, 11

ONE MAY HAVE THE GIFT OF PREACHING WITH
WISDOM GIVEN HIM BY THE SPIRIT; ANOTHER
MAY HAVE THE GIFT OF PREACHING INSTRUC-
TION GIVEN HIM BY THE SAME SPIRIT; AND
ANOTHER THE GIFT OF FAITH GIVEN BY THE
SAME SPIRIT; ANOTHER AGAIN THE GIFT OF
HEALING, THROUGH THIS ONE SPIRIT... ALL
THESE ARE THE WORK OF ONE AND THE SAME
SPIRIT, WHO DISTRIBUTES DIFFERENT GIFTS TO
DIFFERENT PEOPLE JUST AS HE CHOOSES.

I CORINTHIANS 13: 4 - 7

LOVE IS ALWAYS PATIENT AND KIND; IT IS
NEVER JEALOUS; LOVE IS NEVER BOASTFUL
OR CONCEITED; IT IS NEVER RUDE OR SELFISH;
IT DOES NOT TAKE OFFENSE, AND IS NOT
RESENTFUL. LOVE TAKES NO PLEASURE IN
OTHER PEOPLE'S SINS BUT DELIGHTS IN THE
TRUTH; IT IS ALWAYS READY TO EXCUSE, TO
TRUST, TO HOPE AND TO ENDURE WHATEVER
COMES.

2 CORINTHIANS 5: 19

IN OTHER WORDS, GOD IN CHRIST WAS RECON-
CILING THE WORLD TO HIMSELF, NOT HOLD-
ING MEN'S FAULTS AGAINST THEM, AND HE
HAS ENTRUSTED TO US THE NEWS THAT THEY
ARE RECONCILED.

2 CORINTHIANS 13: 4 - 5

YES, BUT HE WAS CRUCIFIED THROUGH WEAK-
NESS, AND STILL HE LIVES NOW THROUGH THE
POWER OF GOD. SO THEN, WE ARE WEAK, AS
HE WAS, BUT WE SHALL LIVE WITH HIM,
THROUGH THE POWER OF GOD, FOR YOUR
BENEFIT. EXAMINE YOURSELVES TO MAKE
SURE YOU ARE IN THE FAITH; TEST YOUR-
SELVES. DO YOU ACKNOWLEDGE THAT JESUS
CHRIST IS REALLY IN YOU? IF NOT, YOU HAVE
FAILED THE TEST.

GALATIANS 4: 6 - 7

THE PROOF THAT YOU ARE SONS IS THAT GOD
HAS SENT THE SPIRIT OF HIS SON INTO OUR
HEARTS: THE SPIRIT THAT CRIES, "ABBA,
FATHER," AND IT IS THIS THAT MAKES YOU A
SON, YOU ARE NOT A SLAVE ANY MORE; AND IF
GOD HAS MADE YOU SON, THEN HE HAS MADE
YOU HEIR.

GALATIANS 5: 1

WHEN CHRIST FREED US, HE MEANT US TO
REMAIN FREE. STAND FIRM, THEREFORE, AND
DO NOT SUBMIT AGAIN TO THE YOKE OF
SLAVERY.

EPHESIANS 1: 4 - 5

BEFORE THE WORLD WAS MADE, HE CHOSE US,
CHOSE US IN CHRIST, TO BE HOLY AND SPOT-
LESS, AND TO LIVE THROUGH LOVE IN HIS
PRESENCE, DETERMINING THAT WE SHOULD
BECOME HIS ADOPTED SONS, THROUGH JESUS
CHRIST FOR HIS OWN KIND PURPOSES,

EPHESIANS 1: 13 - 14

NOW YOU TOO, IN HIM, HAVE HEARD THE MES-
SAGE OF THE TRUTH AND THE GOOD NEWS OF
YOUR SALVATION, AND HAVE BELIEVED IT; AND
YOU TOO HAVE BEEN STAMPED WITH THE SEAL
OF THE HOLY SPIRIT OF THE PROMISE, THE
PLEDGE OF OUR INHERITANCE WHICH BRINGS
FREEDOM FOR THOSE WHOM GOD HAS TAKEN
FOR HIS OWN, TO MAKE HIS GLORY PRAISED.

EPHESIANS 1: 18

MAY HE ENLIGHTEN THE EYES OF YOUR MNID
SO THAT YOU CAN SEE WHAT HOPE HIS CALL
HOLDS FOR YOU, WHAT RICH GLORIES HE HAS
PROMISED THE SAINTS WILL INHERIT.

EPHESIANS 3: 12

THIS IS WHY WE ARE BOLD ENOUGH TO
APPROACH GOD IN COMPLETE CONFIDENCE,

THROUGH OUR FAITH IN HIM; SO, I BEG YOU,
NEVER LOSE CONFIDENCE JUST BECAUSE OF
THE TRIALS THAT I GO THROUGH ON YOUR
ACCOUNT; THEY ARE YOUR GLORY.

EPHESIANS 3: 16 - 20

OUT OF HIS INFINITE GLORY, MAY HE GIVE
YOU THE POWER THROUGH HIS SPIRIT FOR
YOUR HIDDEN SELF TO GROW STRONG, SO
THAT CHRIST MAY LIVE IN YOUR HEARTS
THROUGH FAITH, AND THEN, PLANTED IN
LOVE AND BUILT ON LOVE, YOU WILL WITH
ALL THE SAINTS HAVE STRENGTH TO GRASP
THE BREADTH AND THE LENGTH, THE HEIGHT
AND THE DEPTH; UNTIL, KNOWING THE LOVE
OF CHRIST, WHICH IS BEYOND ALL KNOWL-
EDGE, YOU ARE FILLED WITH THE UTTER
FULLNESS OF GOD. GLORY BE TO HIM WHOSE
POWER, WORKING IN US, CAN DO INFINITELY
MORE THAN WE CAN ASK OR IMAGINE.

EPHESIANS 4: 23 - 24

YOUR MIND MUST BE RENEWED BY A SPIRITU-
AL REVOLUTION SO THAT YOU CAN PUT ON
THE NEW SELF THAT HAS BEEN CREATED IN
GOD'S WAY, IN THE GOODNESS AND HOLINESS
OF THE TRUTH.

EPHESIANS 5: 8 - 9

YOU WERE DARKNESS ONCE, BUT NOW YOU
ARE LIGHT IN THE LORD; BE LIKE CHILDREN
OF LIGHT, FOR THE EFFECTS OF THE LIGHT
ARE SEEN IN COMPLETE GOODNESS AND
RIGHT LIVING AND TRUTH.

PHILIPPIANS 1: 9

MY PRAYER IS THAT YOUR LOVE FOR EACH
OTHER MAY INCREASE MORE AND MORE, AND
NEVER STOP IMPROVING YOUR KNOWLEDGE
AND DEEPENING YOUR PERCEPTION SO YOU
CAN ALWAYS RECOGNIZE WHAT IS BEST.

PHILIPPIANS 4: 11 - 13

I HAVE LEARNED TO MANAGE ON WHATEVER I HAVE. I KNOW HOW TO BE POOR AND I KNOW HOW TO BE RICH TOO. I HAVE BEEN THROUGH MY INITIATION AND NOW I AM READY FOR ANYTHING ANYWHERE: FULL STOMACH OR EMPTY STOMACH, POVERTY OR PLENTY.

COLOSSIANS 2: 14

HE HAS OVERRIDDEN THE LAW, AND CAN-CELLED EVERY RECORD OF THE DEBT THAT WE HAD TO PAY; HE HAS DONE AWAY WITH IT BY NAILING IT TO THE CROSS.

COLOSSIANS 3: 12 - 15

YOU ARE GOD'S CHOSEN RACE, HIS SAINTS; HE LOVES YOU AND YOU SHOULD BE CLOTHED IN SINCERE COMPASSION, IN KINDNESS AND HUMILITY, GENTLENESS AND PATIENCE. BEAR WITH ONE ANOTHER; FORGIVE EACH OTHER AS SOON AS A QUARREL BEGINS. THE LORD HAS FORGIVEN YOU; NOW YOU MUST DO THE SAME. OVER ALL THESE CLOTHES, TO KEEP THEM TOGETHER AND COMPLETE THEM, PUT ON LOVE. AND MAY THE PEACE OF CHRIST REIGN IN YOUR HEARTS, BECAUSE IT IS FOR THIS THAT YOU WERE CALLED TOGETHER AS PARTS OF ONE BODY. ALWAYS BE THANKFUL.

I THESSALONIANS 5: 16

BE HAPPY AT ALL TIMES. PRAY CONSTANTLY AND FOR ALL THINGS GIVE THANKS TO GOD.

II THESSALONIANS 2: 13 - 14

BUT WE FEEL THAT WE MUST BE CONTINUAL-LY THANKING GOD FOR YOU, BROTHERS WHOM THE LORD LOVES, BECAUSE GOD CHOSE YOU FROM THE BEGINNING TO BE SAVED BY THE SANCTIFYING SPIRIT AND BY FAITH IN THE TRUTH. THROUGH THE GOOD NEWS THAT WE BROUGHT HE CALLED YOU TO

THIS SO THAT YOU SHOULD SHARE THE GLORY
OF OUR LORD JESUS CHRIST.

1 TIMOTHY 6: 15 - 16

WHO AT THE DUE TIME WILL BE REVEALED BY
GOD, THE BLESSED AND ONLY RULER OF ALL,
THE KING OF KINGS AND THE LORD OF LORDS,
WHO ALONE IS IMMORTAL, WHOSE HOME IS IN
INACCESSIBLE LIGHT, WHOM NO MAN HAS
SEEN AND NO MAN IS ABLE TO SEE: TO HIM BE
HONOR AND EVERLASTING POWER.

2 TIMOTHY 1: 9 - 10

THIS GRACE HAD ALREADY BEEN GRANTED TO
US, IN CHRIST JESUS, BEFORE THE BEGINNING
OF TIME, BUT IT HAS ONLY BEEN REVEALED
BY THE APPEARING OF OUR SAVIOR CHRIST
JESUS. HE ABOLISHED DEATH, AND HE HAS
PROCLAIMED LIFE AND IMMORTALITY
THROUGH THE GOOD NEWS;

2 TIMOTHY 4: 6 - 8

AS FOR ME, MY LIFE IS ALREADY BEING
POURED AWAY AS A LIBATION, AND THE TIME
HAS COME FOR ME TO BE GONE. I HAVE
FOUGHT THE GOOD FIGHT TO THE END; I HAVE
RUN THE RACE TO THE FINISH; I HAVE KEPT
THE FAITH; ALL THERE IS TO COME NOW IS
THE CROWN OF RIGHTEOUSNESS RESERVED
FOR ME, WHICH THE LORD, THE RIGHTEOUS
JUDGE, WILL GIVE TO ME ON THAT DAY; AND
NOT ONLY TO ME BUT TO ALL THOSE WHO
HAVE LONGED FOR HIS APPEARING.

TITUS 3: 4 - 7

BUT WHEN THE KINDNESS AND LOVE OF GOD
OUR SAVIOR FOR MANKIND WERE REVEALED,
IT WAS NOT BECAUSE HE WAS CONCERNED
WITH ANY RIGHTEOUS ACTIONS WE MIGHT
HAVE DONE OURSELVES; IT WAS FOR NO REA-
SON EXCEPT HIS OWN COMPASSION THAT HE

SAVED US, BY MEANS OF THE CLEANSING
WATER OF REBIRTH AND BY RENEWING US
WITH THE HOLY SPIRIT WHICH HE HAS SO GEN-
EROUSLY POURED OVER US THROUGH JESUS
CHRIST OUR SAVIOR. HE DID THIS SO THAT WE
SHOULD BE JUSTIFIED BY HIS GRACE, TO
BECOME HEIRS LOOKING FORWARD TO INHER-
ITING ETERNAL LIFE. THIS IS DOCTRINE THAT
YOU CAN RELY ON.

HEBREWS 6:11 - 12

OUR ONE DESIRE IS THAT EVERY ONE OF YOU
SHOULD GO ON SHOWING THE SAME EARNEST-
NESS TO THE END, TO THE PERFECT FULFILL-
MENT OF OUR HOPES, NEVER GROWING CARE-
LESS, BUT IMITATING THOSE WHO HAVE THE
FAITH AND THE PERSEVERANCE TO INHERIT
THE PROMISES.

1 PETER 1: 8 - 9

YOU DID NOT SEE HIM, YET YOU LOVE HIM; AND
STILL WITHOUT SEEING HIM, YOU ARE ALREADY
FILLED WITH A JOY SO GLORIOUS THAT IT CAN-
NOT BE DESCRIBED, BECAUSE YOU BELIEVE;
AND YOU ARE SURE OF THE END TO WHICH
YOUR FAITH LOOKS FORWARD, THAT IS, THE
SALVATION OF YOUR SOULS.

1 JOHN 3: 1 - 2

THINK OF THE LOVE THAT THE FATHER HAS
LAVISHED ON US, BY LETTING US BE CALLED
GOD'S CHILDREN; AND THAT IS WHAT WE ARE.
BECAUSE THE WORLD REFUSED TO ACKNOWL-
EDGE HIM, THEREFORE IT DOES NOT
ACKNOWLEDGE US. MY DEAR PEOPLE, WE ARE
ALREADY THE CHILDREN OF GOD BUT WHAT
WE ARE TO BE IN THE FUTURE HAS NOT YET
BEEN REVEALED; ALL WE KNOW IS, THAT
WHEN IT IS REVEALED WE SHALL BE LIKE HIM
BECAUSE WE SHALL SEE HIM AS HE REALLY IS.

I JOHN 4: 18

IN LOVE THERE CAN BE NO FEAR, BUT FEAR IS
DRIVEN OUT BY PERFECT LOVE: BECAUSE TO
FEAR IS TO EXPECT PUNISHMENT, AND ANY-
ONE WHO IS AFRAID IS STILL IMPERFECT IN
LOVE.

REVELATION 21: 3 - 4

THEN I HEARD A LOUD VOICE CALL FROM THE
THRONE, "YOU SEE THIS CITY? HERE GOD
LIVES AMONG MEN. HE WILL MAKE HIS HOME
AMONG THEM; THEY SHALL BE HIS PEOPLE,
AND HE WILL BE THEIR GOD; HIS NAME IS
GOD-WITH-THEM. HE WILL WIPE AWAY ALL
TEARS FROM THEIR EYES; THERE WILL BE NO
MORE DEATH, AND NO MORE MOURNING OR
SADNESS. THE WORLD OF THE PAST HAS
GONE."

SECOND WEEK

FIRST DAY

101. FIRST CONTEMPLATION
THE INCARNATION

JOHN 1: 1 - 18; LUKE 1: 26 - 38 # 262

After the preparatory prayer and three preludes there are three points and a colloquy.

Pray the usual preparatory prayer.

102. FIRST PRELUDE

Calling to mind the history of the Incarnation. Picture the Three Divine Persons before time began. See how They relate to one another and Their deliberations that They might share Who They are with other beings. You might imagine the discussion at the divine table one evening as one of the Persons announces that He would like to become human like those who are about to be formed. He wants to see what it would be like to live by faith, without seeing God face to face, even though it would be a relatively brief time before each creature would rejoin God in the eternal kingdom. Envision the Father and the Holy Spirit amazed at the love that "this second person" expresses in wanting to share His life by dwelling humanly among creation. And the Father too loved the world so much that He created every person in the image and likeness of Himself. God guaranteed that each one would have eternal life and eternal love, and the Spirit would enter each heart, so each person would be able to grow in wisdom and grace. When their temporal life would end they would be completely one with the Trinity.

In the fullness of time and in a moment of time the Second Person would become flesh in the womb of a woman. A message was sent. God realized that if a God-like person went to earth it would be a great example of how a person could act within the structure of time and with the restrictions of human nature. Could one succeed in the face of rejection, sufferings and ignorance, surrounded by trials, oppression and injustice to the very end? A child will lead them; Jesus would show the way. When the Father sent the Son it was a mixture of sadness and joy. Love often brings tears. And such a great love for creation and for others brought a flood of tears.

103. SECOND PRELUDE
Picture the place, see the world at that time, then the province of Galilee in particular. Then focus on the residence of Mary and the details of the scene.

104. THIRD PRELUDE
Ask for what you desire. Here it will be to experience an intimate knowledge of our Lord, with love that is shown not just in select and singular deeds but on a daily ordinary basis. Understand God's way of loving in all situations. How does God love all people: the devout, the casual, even the hostile? Nothing sways God's love from man. See how grace, goodness and truth can illumine even the darkest minds, raise up the most oppressed persons, pacify even the most violent of nations. God's grace conquers all. We pray for intimate knowledge of Jesus.

105. NOTE
In each of these meditations the same preparatory prayer is performed. It reminds me of my relationship with God, my presence to God and God's presence to me. It is important to spend a few moments recalling the history of the scene on which I am about to meditate, whether it is picturing the Trinity before the world was created, the village of Nazareth or whatever is most helpful. Finally, request the special grace for the meditation.

106. FIRST POINT
See the extremes that exist among people of poverty and wealth, sickness and health, war and peace, oppressed and oppressors; see those being born and those dying, those weeping and those laughing.

See the Divine Persons looking upon the face of the earth and beholding the greed and ignorance, the lack of perception, those who are instilling fear and those who are threatened. See the weak-hearted, the kind-hearted and the incredible beauty in gestures of generosity. The Creator looks down and observes all creation to which He has given life. See what God sees, what God has done.

Consider Mary and her call, the announcement that she would bring about the salvation of many, that she would be the hand-maid of the Lord, and that God's good will would be done through her. Reflect on these things.

107. SECOND POINT

Listen quietly and hear what concerns individuals throughout the world, in every country, region and home. How similar are their daily concerns! How typical, how predictable, how much alike they are!

Then hear the Divine Persons speak to each other about Their own creatures, Their own works of art. Listen to Them speak of Incarnation and Redemption, how They talk of giving people grace, spirit and happiness. I wonder if They were searching to find a way of eliminating all war, all violence, even all judgment and yet still have the limitations of created nature? What do you hear Them saying? Listen closely.

Then listen to the exchange between Mary and the angelic messenger. What was in the heart and on the lips of Mary as she heard the clear message of God? Can one experience a new creation, a new lease on life, a completely new career in a single moment? Mary did. Can you?

108. THIRD POINT

Consider the people on the face of the earth: what are the actions of people worldwide, how do they spend their lives? What are the works so common to mankind?

Consider what the Divine Persons do. Can you picture the work of God now, a living God that acts and is act, that loves and is love?

Picture what Mary does as she responds to this extraordinary invitation. Why would a person of such humble stature be selected to be a compassionate, redeeming factor in her world, a world so similar to other generations and other cultures? See Mary's humility and appreciation in her demeanor, words and actions.

In meditating on these points see if you can draw fruit from each of these details.

109. COLLOQUY

Think what you would say to the Divine Persons after having seen, listened and understood the actions that you reflected on during this meditation. Think what you would say to Jesus, the Word Incarnate, and what you would convey to Mary.

Now share what you feel in the presence of the Trinity, in the presence of Jesus and in the presence of Mary. What light have

you received? What greater understanding has come to you?
What grace would you like to ask for? How would you like to
express the love of God that resides in you?

Close with an Our Father.

110. SECOND CONTEMPLATION
THE NATIVITY

LUKE 2: 1 - 14 # 264

Begin with the usual preparatory prayer, the awareness of God's
presence and the offering of my intentions and actions for the
service of God. It is fitting to offer my life in service for God who
has served me and is still serving me. I am God's work of art at
this moment where He gives me life, in the past which He has
redeemed and in the future where He will provide for me. For
right now God is present to me and I am simply and unalterably
present to God.

111. FIRST PRELUDE

This looks at the history of the mystery of the Nativity. See the
young pregnant woman; imagine her thoughts, appreciation, wonder, doubts and questions. Sometimes you can visualize her contemplating the life within her, feeling blest with the extraordinary
privilege of receiving, carrying and giving life. In this particular
scene Mary is travelling to Bethlehem because of a law, because of
authority - and to be with her husband.

Our lives are so often conditioned by the demands of the past
and the present, influenced by pronouncements on paper, prom-
ulgated through authority, and determined by wealth, power and
tradition.

Authorities demand, laws command, violence enforces burdens on individuals, for the law is not merciful, only God is.
While people have the capacity to be merciful, only certain people are in fact compassionate. There are so many who are ambitious and greedy, that the number of compassionate people is
sorely limited. Authority, whose raison d'être is to be at the service of the common good, is often at the service and even the
whim of the governing.

112. SECOND PRELUDE
Get a mental representation of the place. See in your imagination the way from Nazareth to Bethlehem, the conditions under which Christ was born. Enter into the scene, imagine the sizes, shapes and colors. See the streets, houses and shops.

113. THIRD PRELUDE
What is the grace that you are asking for in this contemplation? If we could only know the love of God and feel God's desire for us! It would soothe and flavor all of life; it would bring light-heartedness into our limited life. It would never consist of indebtedness, obligation or slavery. It would simply be a God-response, as one who loves, and the grace of mutuality, loving one another as God has loved us. What a gift it is to be able to show kindness without pressure, responsiveness without desiring a reward! Graced people do not look for thanks; they are not bothered about being appreciated or even remembered.

114. FIRST POINT
Our Lady and Joseph go from Galilee to Bethlehem in obedience to Caesar. Mary his espoused wife was with child.

See the persons at the scene of the Nativity. Make yourself present at that scene, looking, contemplating and then serving as the opportunity arises. Experience the privilege of being able to serve and the favor of this family's friendship, and the delight when your presence is desired by Mary and Joseph. See the presence of others and delight in the miraculous experience of loving attentiveness.

Spend a few moments slowly receiving from this contemplation, noting your feelings and the fruit you are deriving.

115. SECOND POINT
She brought forth her first-born son and she swathed him round and laid him in a manger. Consider, observe and contemplate what the persons are saying at the Nativity scene. Listen and reflect. What does this do for you?

116. THIRD POINT
There appeared with the angel a great multitude of heavenly host praising God with the words, "Glory to God in the highest."

Consider what the family is doing: relating to one another, journeying and ministering. Notice that all creation has been a gift to you; the sky and stars are decorative wrappings, with ribbons of sun and moon. This immense package called existence has been handmade for you. The present moment and all of history have been visible gifts. This birth, the revealed gift of God's son is an unfathomable gift. Can you believe that Jesus' life, death and resurrection were for you? How precious you are! How loved you are, and yet how fragile and small! This is how great God's love is. Reflect and see what you discover from this contemplation.

117. COLLOQUY

Close with an intimate sharing, a heart to heart expression with one of those present at the Nativity or with the loving God who devised and supervised this special and salvific event.

118. THIRD CONTEMPLATION

This will be a Repetition of the first two exercises: the Incarnation and the Nativity.

As we look at these meditations we review God's plan, God's joy and God's work in creation. How different from God's ways are ours? What does man see, think and plan for, what are his joys, actions and occupations?

It is God who has created life and clothed our spirits making us visible. In Creation God made His plan and His will visible and now through the Incarnation we can be confident that what God has done in Christ He has lovingly created in us.

In this repetition, Ignatius asks us to reflect on the miracle that occurs not just at our birth but during each day of our lives, for we are the plan at the heart of God, made manifest today. So we are not just reflecting on the Incarnation of Jesus being made flesh. We observe its recurrence in newborn infants, in people who have been renewed, in our own lives.

In the second exercise, we see the visible expression of God's spirit in parents who give birth and in those who bring life to others. The unity and bond of such a family is a miracle to behold; as God has given life we also give life; as God is one, we also have the gift of unifying. As God cherishes creating and relating, a family that shares and relates is the transparent delight of God.

As we see, hear, feel and taste life around us as often as possible, we become an integral part of the life that we were meant to have. This is how we become like God. These are the profound moments of Nativity as we give birth to an all new day. The peace of God that was passed on to man in the Incarnation is the peace that is present in parents at the birth of a child. The unity that is felt in moments of affection and intimacy, the completeness and satisfaction of ecstasy and contemplation can be found in family and community, in serving and in being served. This is the kingdom that was meant to be; this is God dwelling among us.

Consider the consolation that this meditation has occasioned. Let yourself be captured and delighted by any new understanding and clarity that you discover.

Then look through these two exercises to see where you have been challenged, where there might have been pain. Prior to discovery there is search and risk. In coming to new ideas, along with openness and dialogue, there is vulnerability and grieving if only for the loss of former ways. This also occurs in prayer, it is not always consolation and light. The struggle to arrive at a new level may be compared to an emotional or intellectual teething, like giving birth to a new creation - painful, but so very precious.

Close this exercise with a colloquy and an Our Father.

119. NOTE

In this repetition and in the succeeding ones, follow the same order as in the repetitions of the first week: the preparatory prayer, centering yourself and becoming aware of your presence to God in the here and now. Focus on the intentions of your heart for this meditation at hand. Then go through each of the preludes: memory, history and place. Listen carefully to the grace that you desire.

120. FOURTH CONTEMPLATION

This will consist in a Repetition of the first two exercises, using the same format as in the Repetition above. The purpose of this contemplation is to draw more fruit and nourishment from the first and second exercise. Take your time selecting and emphasizing those discoveries that were most stimulating and helpful. You will be making significant connections for your personal life, and surprisingly new graces will be experienced.

121. FIFTH CONTEMPLATION

Apply your five senses to the material of the first and second contemplations. After the preparatory prayer and the three preludes, involve your senses in the drama unfolding before you. Using one sense at a time will allow the variety of your perceptions to cooperate in heightening your personal involvement. The contemplation will truly become your own, as you enter fully into the mystery.

122. FIRST POINT

In your imagination see the persons and the circumstances of the first two contemplations, the Incarnation and the Nativity, indicating the details and drawing fruit.

123. SECOND POINT

Hear what the people are saying or what they might say. What might you add to the conversation? Draw profit from your presence and attentiveness.

124. THIRD POINT

Smell and taste the infinite fragrance of the Divinity's love for you. Relish the love that is so attractive in the Nativity scene. Savor the truth that you are spirit in flesh and that this familial love is being born in you again and again.

125. FOURTH POINT

Touch and feel what you have seen and heard and tasted. Embrace the persons who love and have loved you. Feel the intimacy that draws you, that makes life worthwhile and fills you with a Godly feeling.

126. COLLOQUY

Share with Mary; speak from your heart to the Incarnate Word and with the Persons of the Trinity. End this contemplation with an Our Father.

ADDITIONAL DIRECTIONS FOR THE SECOND WEEK

127. NOTE I

Throughout this section of the Exercises and the subsequent weeks stay with the particular mystery of Christ's life upon which you are meditating. Dismiss any desire to progress to the next experience in Christ's life. There is no rush. There is sufficient grace in each day and in each prayer period.

Sometimes the reason why we wish to do too much at one time is because of some pressure to finish things quickly, or because of a desire to be productive and efficient. God and love are beyond all measure of time. It is normal to want to move on; just remember that there is no getting ahead with God.

There is a normal tendency to compare and make efforts to be the best. However, with God, each day is a gift perfectly suited to you. There is no need to think about the comparative or competitive best with your God and Father. You are especially called into the world on this day to be a light for the world, so there is no need to measure what you could do in the future or have done in the past. This is the light that gives true direction and warmth.

People may also want to do more or to move on. When people enjoy something they have a natural tendency to want more. Curiosity is also part of our natural make-up. Each one's level of boredom and interest varies greatly, depending on factors like previous conditioning, assumed values and the influence of others. So as we meditate on one mystery at a time we realize that each particular grace is sufficient.

128. NOTE II

There are five different chances to meditate on the Incarnation, to bring our sensitivity and our various moods to prayer. The equivalent of a full day's reflection and spiritual exercises is given to this central mystery of Christianity.

Ignatius reiterates in annotation # 72 about the times for prayer before meals, before bedtime, upon rising and before or after Mass. These are natural breaks in the day or rhythms of a person's life and provide fewer interruptions and more concrete signals for prayer times. However, the times that you discover are most conducive are actually the best times to pray. There is certainly a value in praying at different times of the day about the same text. Even though the meditation's theme might be identical, notice how your experiences and your reactions vary.

129. NOTE III

The director needs to be aware whether the retreatant is finding the length and frequency of prayer time interesting and meaningful. If not, together you can decide what adjustments need to be made. After a new contemplation, the Repetition follows, then an Application of the Senses is used, not as a test, trial or discipline but simply to derive greater fruit for the retreatant. Ignatius is also reminding the retreatant and the director to be sensitive to whether praying late at night or early in the morning is effective and joyful, or in fact burdensome and self-defeating. Is it seen as an opportunity or a sacrifice? This note reminds the director to keep track of the schedule and the relative merit of the entire process.

130. NOTE IV

Of the ten Additional Directions # 73 - 82 given during the First Week, there are a few recommended changes for this Second Week.

In annotation # 74, it was important during the First Week to realize and admit that I had been living an illusion. That somehow I needed to find a way to come to my senses and be able to see through my ignorant and unrealistic ideas. My fervent prayer was to "wake-up". In this Second Week my attitude is to concentrate on the particular meditation I am considering rather than focusing on my own limitations. Now I desire to know the Eternal Word and the security of God's love in order to serve and follow more closely.

Annotation # 78 invited me to contemplate on the particular mystery of the life of Christ in a special way. In the First Week I was not concentrating on the consolation of Jesus' life but rather admitting how easily I had been misled. I may have realized that I had been fooled and even admitted my need for someone to take the scales from my eyes. In this Second week we are looking right at Jesus with our eyes filled with truth and wonder. And I see the answer before me.

In the First Week annotation # 79 recommended withdrawing

from your familiar world and letting go of your past to get a fresh perspective. During this Second Week you will find yourself adjusting the room, lighting, your whole environment and place of prayer whether inside or outside to enhance your meditation on the life of Christ. Make use of the weather and your diet; notice your spirit finding nourishment in different foods and situations; observe yourself becoming more joyful. You might find it helpful to review the Additions with the changes noted here.

131. NOTE V

As you approach each prayer exercise, recall your intentions for this prayer period and sum up the particular points for the exercise you are about to do. Then just prior to your prayer, for the space of an Our Father consider Jesus full of affection and admiration standing next to you. Then begin your prayer.

SECOND DAY

132. FIRST CONTEMPLATION
THE PRESENTATION

LUKE 2: 22 - 39 # 268

FIRST POINT. Joseph and Mary took Jesus up to Jerusalem to present Him to the Lord. Every first-born male must be consecrated.

SECOND POINT. Simeon took Jesus into his arms and blessed God, "Now you can let your servant go in peace."

THIRD POINT. Anna the prophetess spoke of the Child to all who looked forward to the deliverance of Jerusalem.

SECOND CONTEMPLATION
THE FLIGHT INTO EGYPT

MATTHEW 2: 13 - 18 # 269

FIRST POINT. Herod wished to kill the newborn child. The message arrived for Joseph to take mother and child and flee into Egypt.

SECOND POINT. Joseph arose by night and fled to Egypt.

THIRD POINT. Jesus remained in exile there until the death of Herod.

The Repetition exercises and the Application of the Senses meditation will be made as was done on the preceding day.

While children need the security of a loving home, they have an unfolding destiny to go out to the world, to be part of that bigger world. Jesus' ritual presentation involved a premature insertion in the problems and suffering of the world. The gratitude of Simeon and the prophesy by Anna thrust this young family into the mystery of salvation and rejection. The mixture of life that each one endures was there from the outset of Jesus' infancy. The Flight into Egypt depicts the struggle and the separation that is part of human suffering. Flight and exile are still powerful experiences whether they are necessitated by natural catastrophes or by man's decrees. The pressure of the law, the threat of power, the fear of those who govern with rigidity and violence are as real today as in the time of Jesus.

133. NOTE

Sometimes it is important to modify your schedule depending on what you desire. During the Second Week there are specific things to be desired as you ponder the Life of Christ. Discover which changes will bring the most benefit.

THIRD DAY

134. FIRST CONTEMPLATION
THE LIFE OF JESUS
AGE TWELVE TO THIRTY

LUKE 2: 51 - 52 # 271

FIRST POINT. See the maturity, courage and freedom of Jesus speaking with the doctors of the Law about the meaning of the scriptures.

SECOND POINT. Juxtapose Jesus' attitude of reverence and obedience toward His parents while being very conscious of his maturing in age, wisdom and grace.

THIRD POINT. Discover the combination of Jesus working alongside His father, Joseph and applying Himself to His new vocation, the new work of His heavenly Father.

SECOND CONTEMPLATION
JESUS IN THE TEMPLE
AT AGE TWELVE

LUKE 2: 41 - 50 # 272

FIRST POINT. Jesus goes with his parents to Jerusalem for the feast of Passover.

SECOND POINT. Jesus' parents did not know that Jesus had stayed behind in Jerusalem. They went back and looked for him everywhere.

THE SPIRITUAL EXERCISES

THIRD POINT. After three days they found him in the temple sitting among with the doctors, listening to them and asking them questions.

In these meditations Jesus shows respect for His parents and for the teachers of the temple. While there is respect and reverence there is neither adoration nor submission. There is an understanding of values and there is an expression of love. There is no pretension that the law or obedience can save. The law cannot substitute for one's own unique grace. This was a critical experience for Jesus and may be for us as we meditate on the limited value of authority and law. Let us never confuse righteousness and conformity with grace and vocation.

The second day was a reflection on real life, where we came from, and on God, Who called us to live. With all of our great hopes and ideals, we are called to see with our own eyes and to attempt to understand and experience life fully, even as Jesus did.

Two repetitions and the applications of the senses as on the previous days follow these meditations.

135. THE CONSIDERATION OF THE DIFFERENT STATES OF LIFE

The example which Christ our Lord gave of the First State of life, which is that of observing the Commandments, has already been considered in meditating on His obedience to His parents. This is considered the first State, where you are nourished and supported. By listening to parents and teachers who know the world and you better than you do, you grow in an atmosphere of exploration and learning. Rooted in the holiness of a family that cares for you, you develop naturally, believing that you are valuable and that you are a priority for these people. You have received many signs of love from those who sheltered you, fed you, warmed you and healed you. Believing these visible signs brings about your spiritual growth. So the whole experience of childhood and parenting is the holiness of the First State of Life.

An example of the Second State which Jesus experienced was that of the service of others. Having already experienced the love of family and the confidence which that instills, Jesus was ready for the next stage – to become detached. This meant leaving His family and a departure from His familiar setting, both of which had fostered His earlier growth.

In this Second State, He believed in his own uniqueness, his own loveableness and his own ability to service. He found great joy in bringing his view of life to others and bringing his view of love and community to the world. He did this with the simple instruments at his disposal: his truthful words, compassionate deeds and his personal choice of companions. His variety of works included visiting the marketplace, attending to the sick, consoling the mourning and forgiving sinners. He loved to encourage people to experience the joy in serving. He performed daring gestures as washing peoples' feet, talking to women in public, going to the homes of unpopular people. And so Jesus' life in the Second Stage was one of contemplation, dialogue and service. There seemed to be a unique balance of discovering his gifts and blending them with the needs of the people.

As you continue to investigate and to contemplate Jesus' life, an important question to be asking yourself is, how do you want to spend your time and use your gifts with the many choices that are continuously presented to you? Which is most appealing to you? Being present and nurturing a specific family, or being available and serving those who are not your own in the larger community? What is most desirable to you? This question will keep coming up, so your observation of yourself and your conscious involvement take on an important role in these meditations on the Life of Christ.

Let us consider the intentions of Jesus as we ponder some of His works and deeds. Let us try to get to know the mind of Jesus: what delighted him and what drew him. In contrast we might see some of the things that delight people and the basic things that satisfy them. Then as we see Jesus and some of the world's ways we once again discover the state of life that we wish to choose.

As we contemplate Jesus' life and experience our own reactions, we will be preparing ourselves for truly following our own inspirations.

FOURTH DAY

136. A MEDITATION ON TWO STANDARDS

The Standard of Christ is like the Standard of God Who wants our happiness, Who wants us to be peaceful and joyful, Who wants us to be recognizable as followers of Jesus by one mark – by our love for one another. Christians must be noticed not by numbers of followers nor by wealth or worldly blessings, not by law or rituals or uniforms, but by their acceptance and compassion. This is the Spirit of Christ, this is the standard that Jesus presents. If there could be a flag or standard it would say without any conditions or ulterior motives, "I Love You."

The other standard is the world's standard. The world would like you to serve it, its causes, its philosophies and its decrees. The world's flag would say, "You Obey Me." The world wants you to give up your life, surrender your mind, will and body. The world's way, whether it comes from individuals or churches, nations or military services, all chant the same tune. They want your solemn, lifetime, definitive commitment, so that the world and its various institutional goals will endure and succeed. Their banners imply, "We want you and we want you to depend on us." You are a pawn to serve the ends of others, whether it is a military dictatorship or one of the many "isms" that exist and enslave in our contemporary society.

PRAYER

The usual preparatory prayer.

137. FIRST PRELUDE

Look at the history of the world. The way, the life, the love of Christ on one side and the glamour, the demands, the destructiveness of the world on the other.

138. SECOND PRELUDE

This is a mental representation of the place. Here it will be good to see Jesus in one of the places where many had seen him – on a donkey, on a dirt road, in a village, or in a boat anchored by the shore with people milling about, or sitting on the hillside telling entertaining stories, his warmth and affection so obvious. See Jesus washing little children's feet and everyone laughing and getting in line. See Jesus bathing a sick man's feet. See Jesus anointing a leper's sores. See the people touched, watching and listening, children playing and happy, the laughter, the peace and the sharing of words, food and love. This is the standard of Jesus; this is the standard of community and family; this is reality.

The second thing to look at in this representation of place is a different kind of chief, a different kind of leader, a leader of one of the world's institutions, chairman of the board, CEO, General, President, or modern day chief priest. See the robes, the stately uniform and the distinguished surroundings, the wealthy circumstances, maybe even gold braid is noticeable. Do you sense the power and awe immediately? Can you feel the honor, respect and fear that is visible on the faces of his servants and secretaries? Notice the number of people who strive to do the bidding of this powerful national or international, religious or secular figure? See them reverencing and accommodating this dignitary.

139. THIRD PRELUDE

Ask for what I desire. Here it might be for a true knowledge of the veneer or the ploys of the world, its rewards, privileges and bribes. See if I can understand the true knowledge of the effects of the powerful, wealthy and influential class, so that I will not be fooled or think that my happiness in any way resides in this accumulation of things or in the ability to manipulate.

The second grace to ask for is a true knowledge of the style of Christ. When a person desires to follow Christ's way how does he apply it, what are the means, how will he be sure of his direction? What a wonderful grace to be able to sense the overflowing love of God for his people and to feel the desires and responses that it creates in me!

FIRST PART
THE STANDARD OF THE WORLD

140. FIRST POINT

You might imagine the conference room, the "War" room, where day after day military people are planning their offense and defense, the destruction of God's people, God's family. Irrationally and ironically they use God's creation, things and people to destroy other people and things. What utter nonsense! What are the people gathered around this table seeking to gain for themselves at the enormous cost and sacrifice of human lives – territory, prestige, medals? Do they believe they are winning something meaningful, or achieving some ideal by killing people of other persuasions? Do they sincerely believe they are bringing good to the world or liberating people by destroying people?

See the power emanating from the chair of the secretary of defense, or from the chief of the armed forces, see the power of the military leaders, or the so-called National Security Administrations. See the millions of people at their literal disposal and the number of young boys who will do their bidding without question, out of fear or for a prize. See the manipulation and the capacity for destruction of individuals and of whole cultures at this one table. Hear the demands for justice and revenge, vengeance and punishment from the officials present. See the plans for victory and demise and the promises for glory via intolerable suffering. Witness the prospects for violence among the innocent, the families, the Third World – always the Third World.

See the connection between the obsession for control and wealth with the addiction to power and influence. See clearly the standard of the world, its potential destructiveness when placed in the hands of greedy people. They need great might to protect their fortune. Their kingdom is of this world, not for the benefit of mankind, but simply to dominate. They would never sacrifice their lives but they will readily sacrifice the unknown soldier and the nameless poor to protect their personal investments and interests.

SECOND POINT

See the effect throughout the world of just one committee from one country, and the mercenaries, the spies, the agents, the undercover people serving the interests of this one committee.

THIRD POINT

Consider how the leader at the head of the table ensnares them ever so politely. How he goads them! There is competition, comparison. Their jobs are at stake by the bidding of one person; their reputation, their stature and their future is jeopardized or flourishes with each one's reaction. They understand that if they leave the service or the office they would be a threat to the establishment; they would be considered dangerous. They discover quickly there is no turning back. They either kill for the duration of their tenure or are killed.

See their plight – their lives and options are sorely limited. These so-called powerful people are marked men, without freedom and with no exit. So they survive by marking others for death and destruction.

See the poor who are being used through conscription, through the use of threats, through the development of an addiction. They are first tempted with riches that they might covet them, then they are seduced by the empty honors and false power of this world. Once they are bribed by medals of approval they come to an overweening pride. The gleam of the world's rewards soon blinds their eyes, then freezes the heart, and pride finally decapitates the individual.

And so the first step will be riches, the second is honor and third is pride. This is the Standard of the World and these are the means as well as the ends. There is no more. Yet these inducements are overwhelming for the unspiritual. The deprived will be easily seduced. People who believe that they do not possess the Kingdom, or that their God is not all-gentle, all-generous and all-merciful, can easily be cajoled. The riches of life seem more appealing than the love of God. For those who do not realize they have the kingdom and the infinite riches of God's love, material possessions give them their only sense of security.

The fallacious honors of victory and prestige do not feed the body or soul. When people do not have love for each other they look for praise in accomplishments and in the estimation of others. Their sole nourishment comes from recognition, adulation and the salutes from other fearful people. These officials are trapped on a precarious staircase bearing temporary titles. They are on steps that demand not only their dedication but their souls as well. In the ascent, destruction, suffering and conquering are the only legacy to their credit. And the poverty of the world continues. This has been the history of the world. This is the world's way. This is called a Standard – it is real, it is sad, yet it is not uncommon; in fact, it is popular.

SECOND PART

143. THE STANDARD OF CHRIST

Picture Jesus and the kind of a leader He is. What style of leadership do you notice in Jesus as He stands with people gathered around him? Notice how they talk about the day's affairs and how they share their desires and how they question one another. What is the style of Jesus' leadership as He sits and talks with people about their personal concerns: farming and their crops, fishing and their catch, their families and the health of their children. See Jesus the compassionate and understanding one who can identify with every strata of society for He is gentle and humble of heart. His authentic interest in people and his blatant displays of freedom and wisdom draw people in ever greater numbers.

144. FIRST POINT

Consider Jesus in a particular place, in His outward appearance, how do you see Him? Can you see His eyes and His looks and His expressions and can you hear the tone of His voice? Can you observe the people and what His presence does for them?

145. SECOND POINT

Consider how Jesus attracts people to listen to His words and how he challenges them to question and think for themselves. Jesus is a leader who uses neither law nor power, and never resorts to violence. He does not use lobbies or alliances, nor does he make deals. He came to give to all people His message, His deeds and Himself. He passed on a way of conflict resolution, a way of forgiveness and communication. What a lovely manner He had, as He chose, invited and welcomed people! He seemed to be a person without bias or prejudice. How can this be? How can He be so clear and true with each person so that each person feels favored and special, as if God Himself had whispered "I love you" in each one's heart, singularly and deliberately? No one was ever excluded, or ever felt excluded, or ever could be excluded from this love.

146. THIRD POINT

Listen to the address Jesus makes to His friends as He sends them on an enterprise to reach out to others just as He had reached out to them. See these disciples with their hearts overflowing with spirit and joy. Jesus helped people believe in themselves by first telling them that they had talents and goodness beyond their wildest dreams. Jesus could see their gifts as clearly as one observes the sky and sea. He convinced people that their presence was so powerful that they could heal the sick, warm the coldhearted and eliminate fear from just about anyone. This made their hearts dance. On one occasion He said to them, "You and I are one," and on another, all the gifts you see in Me you have. In John's gospel Jesus overwhelmed them by saying, "of all the works that you have seen Me do, you shall do greater ones." They could not wait to try it out. Were they really that special, that good and that loved? As they went on their way Jesus reminded them that they were free to enjoy their gifts, to enjoy God's love whenever they so desired. He told them not to worry about giving without measure for there would be no end to His blessings. They might be tired emotionally and physically but there would be no end to the graces that they were receiving and sharing. Jesus got people to believe that even with little or none of the world's goods the kingdom of God was present, and vital in and through them. Rejoice!

Jesus taught his friends and listeners not to be disappointed or discouraged by the world's obsessions, its need for power, its insatiable greed. He taught them not to be offended when people did not appreciate them. He gave them simple things to meditate on so they would not be hindered by worry, "Look at the birds...observe the lilies." He then gave them approaches to use by which He encouraged his disciples.

First, appreciate life as the most precious of gifts, and see wealth, power and pride as superficial realities. Resent no one and always be ready to understand and accept.

Second, understand that being insulted or being passed over would never diminish the truth that the kingdom is yours and you are singularly favored by God. Know that insults come from the conditioned person's head and mouth and they are the irrevocable possession of the insulter. Honors are not to be aspired to, for these passing thrills are vain and unsatisfying. You will only seek them when you doubt that you are singularly honored by God, who created, redeemed and chose you.

Third, realize that true humility is reached when you are unrecognized by the world and unperturbed by it, when you notice that you no longer seek the recognition of the world and are no longer seduced by the standard of pride, power and privilege.

Can you imagine being fully detached from the need for honors and riches and thoroughly unafraid of rejection and insults? If these virtues can be attained then all other spiritual gifts will come easily, for you will not be controlled. You will be free to follow your heart rather than strive for honors and riches that are available in the world.

147. COLLOQUY

After pondering these ideas it would be fitting to check to see if they ring true by a dialogue with Mary. How close am I to this standard of Jesus? Maybe in reflecting I will discover that what Jesus loved to do, gives me joy too. Are the people and actions that gave Jesus a sense of peace and satisfaction the things that attract me? What are my preferences and how do they compare with those of Jesus? Am I satisfied with my detachment from the standard of this world or do I feel deprived or insecure? Do I feel the security of a child and realize I possess riches that are beyond measure? Am I happy with myself and my gifts, with my friends and my relationships.

Confer with Mary; ask her to ask Jesus if I have any hidden desires for praise, approval and honor. How free am I to be overlooked, misunderstood and rejected like Christ was? Am I still able to be generous when I sense rejection or failure, or do I tend to become depressed? Am I so confirmed in God's love that I can rejoice in another's success. Do I see clearly that my happiness does not depend on accomplishments? My joy is all the greater when I realize its only source is God and that the supply is endless.

I will end this colloquy with a Hail Mary.

SECOND COLLOQUY

Ask Jesus to obtain this same grace and favor with the same clarity and assurance from the Father. I will then say the "Soul of Christ" prayer.

THIRD COLLOQUY
Ask the Father directly to grant the same graces and then close with an Our Father.

148. NOTE
This exercise will be made twice, with two repetitions and with three colloquies with Our Lady, her Son and the Father. Thus this theme for meditation will be done four times in somewhat different ways. The following meditation on the Three Classes of Men will also be done in a similar way.

149. THREE CLASSES OF PERSONS
This meditation is to teach the retreatant a method for making good choices.

PRAYER
The usual opening prayer.

150. FIRST PRELUDE
This is the history of the three classes of men. Each of them has acquired a large fortune but not entirely for the love of God. Each one of them is feeling the burden that arises from their attachment to the sum acquired which is impeding their peace. So each one wants to rid himself of the burden. The burden is threefold, noticed by the amount of time spent on trying to decide what is right, by anxiety that this might have some value in the future, and by worry about what other people might think. The one thing they are certain about is that this is not bringing peace to their lives.

151. SECOND PRELUDE
This is a representation of the place. You might picture yourself in the presence of God sharing with Him and collaborating with some very special people whom you have loved and trusted. You might prefer an intimate gathering with some dear friends and yourself explaining the situation completely. After hearing the facts what do they tell you? They might initially express their joy in being considered the inner circle of your friends; they would probably remind you of how much you are loved, of how much goodness and joy you bring to life.

With this atmosphere of affection seek to know and desire what brings the most peace.

152. THIRD PRELUDE

This is to ask for what you desire. Ask for the grace to know what decision will bring the most joy and to choose what is best for your own peace of mind. And so while I may have the desire to be alleviated of this burden, I must pray for the courage to choose and act according to my intention. When there is no certain answer, I wish to discover what is more conducive for peace for myself and for the world. If I can see clearly that there is a choice that is more conducive, then my desires will lead to appropriate behavior and action. In this present moment I do not know the future, yet grace will enable me to see clearly. And that is what I am praying for.

153. THE FIRST CLASS

These people would like to rid themselves of the attachment in order to find peace but their life goes by and they never do anything about it. The desire was present and they had good intentions but no decision was made, no resolution and therefore no action ever took place. They are well intentioned people.

154. THE SECOND CLASS

They also want to rid themselves of the attachment so they will find their life more peaceful and harmonious. However, they have an urge to preserve what they have acquired. They would like to possess material goods, but they do not like the anxiety that accompanies this attachment. They are afraid of letting go, or because of some unknown insecurity they persist in clinging. They would truly like to be free but they also want to hold on. They are willing to get some advice on ways of ridding themselves of their negative feelings but they continue to drag this burden with them. They consider numerous options that promise to satisfy both tensions. They ask for the grace to rid themselves of the personal attachment and the gnawing anxiety, but they never ask for the grace to get rid of the acquired sum. They are fearful people.

155. THE THIRD CLASS

This class of persons wants to rid themselves of the attachment and they wish to do so in such a way that they have no desire to retain or to relinquish the sum acquired. The desire is clear, the means are still not clear. This third class of people is open to whatever means are necessary to attain the end. Their intention is purely to follow God's inspirations; they will choose whatever is better for the service of peace and justice. They believe that if they choose what is best for God's people it is God's will.

Meanwhile they strive to conduct themselves as if every attachment to this acquired sum has been broken. So they act as if they are detached, as though the ties are broken and they see how they feel without this dependency or burden. They also make efforts neither to want this particular thing that they acquired, nor anything else in the future, unless the service of God and the good of people will result.

The priority for this Class is the advancement of peace and the service of justice. This affects the acceptance and relinquishing of all things, and the use of all things. This person will check his desires to see if they seem to blend with God's will. This person finds himself motivated by one goal: Eucharistic people serving one another. The goal and the means are the same. And so, in considering various questions, his other attachments are dropped. He has attained the secret of awareness – seeing clearly and living without fear.

156. THREEFOLD COLLOQUY

Make use of the three colloquies employed in the preceding contemplations. Direct these dialogues to Mary, Jesus and the Father. #147

157. NOTE

When we feel the disturbing effects of an attachment Ignatius suggests in this Note that we pray using the Colloquies so that we will choose to serve God with the spirit of detachment. I need to pray for this grace of detachment so that I can be free from any dependencies that include chemical, psychological or other powerful inclinations.

It is a very special grace to be able to see all things in light of the service and praise of God. This grace is expressed by peace reigning in families and communities, by individuals taking one patient step at a time and by the witness of people helping one another.

As the burden of an attachment is admitted, know that there is hope, and a way to freedom is available. You have the power to exert some initial control by patience and prayer.

While attachments have a certain appeal and bring limited pleasure, there is another way that brings lasting joy and a greater good. A sincere desire to have less material things must be based on the happiness I already experienced in having less. Why would anyone want to store glitter? Why would anyone want to stockpile things?

I must ask for the grace to be open, to see clearly, and to respond accurately to my unique vocation. In whatever I do, receiving, retaining or relinquishing, I need to see the beauty and the value in each choice. I might desire peace with the best intentions, and still be like that "First Class of People" who never put grace into action. Therefore I must beg God for the grace to see what I can do, and then do it.

FIFTH DAY

158. THE BAPTISM OF CHRIST
MATTHEW 3: 1-17 #273

FIRST POINT. Jesus came from Galilee to the Jordan to be baptized by John.

SECOND POINT. John tried to dissuade Him, "It is I who need baptism from you and yet you come to me!"

THIRD POINT. As soon as Jesus was baptized the heavens opened and a voice spoke from heaven. "This is my Son, my Beloved; my favor rests on Him."

This contemplation begins with the journey of Christ from Nazareth to the River Jordan and includes Jesus' Baptism.

John wished to excuse himself from baptizing Jesus because he felt unworthy. He gave in after Jesus said, "Leave it like this for the time being."

It might be good to ponder Jesus setting out into a new world and a new career, leaving all the familiar surroundings. He would invite people to share their views with Him and then to share their lives with others.

Jesus had done much good in his own hometown and probably liked his reputation. And now he was choosing a radically different way of life. It included risk, adventure and many unknowns;

it must have often led him to prayer.

Along your own retreat journey, similar notions could be a significant part of your life as you go from one phase of security in establishing yourself, then responding to the risk of an unpredictable vocation. Sometimes the choices involve little change in your work or living conditions, and sometimes dramatic ones.

What is the grace at the center of your heart that fills you with consolation and courage? Maybe taking strolls alongside of a river, or making a retreat would help you to identify with Jesus as you enter this next stage of your life. Jesus was more than halfway through his life when the Spirit called Him to a new ministry. The life expectancy of people in His day was not that long, which gives his mission a special meaning. Jesus probably figured he had a few good years left. His hour had come; it had come on other occasions and it would come again. This was a special time for Jesus and this is a special time for you.

See John the Baptist. One thing that is remarkable is that John the Baptist says that he is unworthy. How appropriate! Every minister of Baptism is unworthy. This is the same message for priests and ministers of the Church and for all the people of God. While we often feel unworthy, we belong to God and by God's design we are innocent forever. We always were and always will be innocent before God.

Hearts and the heavens sing out the Good News that this is the work of the Holy Spirit from the beginning. This is my Beloved child in whom I am infinitely delighted. As each minister approaches to baptize an innocent infant, he announces good news; it is an extraordinary privilege. To be able to say in the Name of God, the Father, Son and Holy Spirit that this is God's child is truly a sacrament, for this child was created and loved by God unalterably and eternally. To announce that this child is innocent and without blame before God and man is an utter joy for the minister to proclaim. It is stating the obvious for those with faith, for God does not judge nor keep a record of sin, so all are innocent through, with and in God. The privilege of performing these visible signs called sacraments is the gift of announcing that creation, love, innocence and redemption are all God's work. Let no one during your lifetime convince you otherwise. You are my beloved in whom I am always well pleased.

NOTES

159. NOTE I

This meditation on the Baptism of Jesus should be contemplated twice, followed by two repetitions and the Application of the Senses. With each exercise begin with the preparatory prayer, follow with the three preludes of history, place and grace and conclude by praying the three colloquies from #147.

160. NOTE II

During these and the succeeding meditations until the end of the Second Week, you might examine the Additional Directions #27 - 31 and #73 - 90. You can use these annotations for your examen during this time.

SIXTH DAY

161. THE TEMPTATION OF CHRIST

LUKE 4: 1 - 13 and MATTHEW 4: 1 - 11 #274

FIRST POINT. Jesus fasted for forty days and forty nights.

SECOND POINT. Jesus was tempted, "Command these stones... Cast thyself down... Worship me."

THIRD POINT. "And angels appeared and looked after Him."

Follow the same order as was given for the Fifth day. There will be five meditations on this theme. After Jesus had been baptized, he went to the desert where he retreated, fasted and prayed. He had recently left home and already dramatic things had begun to happen to Him. He had been recognized by John the Baptist, He had felt the unquestionable favor of God and now there was some special work He wanted to accomplish.

During these days he examined his experiences of the world and reflected on the personal goals for His life. What did He realistically think he could accomplish in the next few years – God willing? In what ways could He achieve them? He began to see His mission clearly.

Although He knew He was being sent as an offering, He felt that the world was being offered to Him. This was His hour. Since Jesus realized what had happened to prophets before him, He reflected on what could happen to Him if He were to choose a certain path. How threatened the rich would be if He preached good news to the poor, how upset theologians would be if he preached equality with both God and man, how angry those in authority would be if he preached freedom and truth!

Jesus was tempted to live up to the expectations of people, to become somebody, to do sensational things to accomplish His mission. Jesus was also tempted to attain the approval and support of all the people, to be praised and glorified, to be acclaimed king, to be a ruler, but Jesus knew the consequences of power and the devastating results of force. The world already had a history of conquerors. Having lived under the Roman Empire and having seen the actions of the chief priests, He experienced the tyranny both of religious authority and military power. So while it seemed justifiable to return evil for evil, to use power to combat power, to make your enemies submit, to achieve your righteous goals by using influence and weaponry, Jesus saw it as a temptation. For Jesus had come on earth as man to live each day as one of us, the least among his brothers and sisters, and to serve each person, the least no less than the greatest.

He chose to feed, to visit and to touch. He chose to do Godly work directly and then He invited others to do the same. He chose not to judge and condemn, but to rescue and save. He did not come to conquer the world, but rather to announce good news to the ends of the earth. The world did not need another conqueror, but it desperately needed one who was capable of loving her. Jesus wanted to be that one. He was.

With this meditation there will be two repetitions and then the Application of the Senses.

SEVENTH DAY

THE VOCATION OF THE APOSTLES
JOHN 1: 35 - 51; #275
LUKE 5: 1 - 28; MATTHEW 4: 18 - 22;
MARK 1: 16 - 2: 14 #161

FIRST POINT. Three stages are evident in the call of Peter and Andrew. a) an invitation to learn of Jesus and his mission, b) an inclination to follow Christ in certain works and situations, c) a decision to follow Christ unconditionally.

SECOND POINT. He called Philip and Matthew and the others.

THIRD POINT. They seem to be uneducated and from a humble condition. Consider the dignity to which they were called. Notice the lack of pressure, no bribes or threats, no ulterior motives in each one's vocation. Consider their courageous gifts and transparent graces.

EIGHTH DAY

THE SERMON ON THE MOUNT
MATTHEW 5: 1 - 48 #278

FIRST POINT. Jesus proposes a series of beatitudes to His disciples, Blessed are the poor, the meek, the merciful, the mourners, the hungry, the pure of heart, the peacemakers, the persecuted. Which are you?

SECOND POINT. He exhorts them to be courageous in their use of talents and inspirations. "Let your light shine before men in order that they may see your good works and glorify your Father in heaven."

THIRD POINT. Jesus explains his new and difficult commandments and closes with, "Love your enemies, and pray for those who persecute you. In this way you will be true children of your Father in heaven, for he causes his sun to rise on good and bad alike."

NINTH DAY

CHRIST WALKS UPON THE LAKE
MATTHEW 14: 22 - 33 #280

FIRST POINT. After sending the crowds away Jesus went up into the hills by himself to pray.

SECOND POINT. Jesus went toward them walking on the lake, and the disciples were terrified.

THIRD POINT. At once Jesus called out to them, "Courage! It is I! Do not be afraid." Peter at His bidding, came to Jesus walking on the water and started sinking. Jesus put out his hand at once and held him. And as they got into the boat the wind ceased.

TENTH DAY

JESUS PREACHES IN THE TEMPLE
LUKE 19: 47 - 48 #288
FIRST POINT. Jesus was teaching in the temple every day.
SECOND POINT. The chief priests and the scribes, with the support of the leading citizens, tried to do away with him.
THIRD POINT. They did not see how they could carry this out because the people as a whole hung on His words.

ELEVENTH DAY

THE RAISING OF LAZARUS
JOHN 11: 1 - 45 #285
FIRST POINT. Mary and Martha sent this message to Jesus, "Lord, the man you love is ill.'
SECOND POINT. On arriving, Jesus found that Lazarus had been in the tomb for four days already. Mary said the same words as Martha, "Lord, if you had been here my brother would not have died."
Jesus said, "I am the resurrection. If anyone believes in me even though he dies he will live."
THIRD POINT. Jesus wept, thanked the Father for hearing His prayer and then said, "Lazarus here! Come out!"

TWELFTH DAY

PALM SUNDAY
MATTHEW 21: 1 - 17 #287
FIRST POINT. Jesus sends two disciples for a donkey and her colt. If anyone questions you, say "The Master needs them and will send them back directly."
SECOND POINT. This took place to fulfill the prophecy of *ISAIAH* 62: 11, "Look your savior comes to you; he is humble, he rides on a donkey."
THIRD POINT. The crowds came forth to meet Jesus, they spread palm branches in the way, shouting, "Hosanna to the Son of David, Blessings on Him who comes in the name of the Lord. Hosanna in the highest heavens!

162. NOTE I

Anyone according to his wishes may lengthen or shorten this Second Week of retreat. If you wish to use other Contemplations with recommended Points and Scripture passages, refer to the Mysteries of the Second Week, Annotations #261 - 288. If you wish to shorten it, you might eliminate whichever ones that have been previously assigned for they serve primarily as an introduction and offer a method for approaching later meditations.

163. NOTE II

The treatment of the matter dealing with the Choice of a Way of Life will begin with the contemplation of our Lord's departure from Nazareth for the Jordan. On the Fifth Day of this Second Week and on the days following, Annotations #169 - 189 can be reflected on while the retreatant is meditating on the Mysteries of the Life of Christ.

164. NOTE III

Before entering upon the Choice of a Way of Life, Annotation #169, and in order to have the attitude of mind that was in Christ Jesus, it will be very useful to consider attentively the following Three Kinds of Humility. These along with the three colloquies should be pondered during each day.

THREE KINDS OF HUMILITY

165. THE FIRST KIND OF HUMILITY

There is a certain kind of humility that all people need for security and in order to preserve their human rights. This first kind consists in seeing the creative hand of God in one's life and in accepting the loving plan of God for all things. God is the Author of life and in charge of life. We were created to live with each other in freedom, with respect, harmony and a fullness of peace. We were created to cooperate, not to dominate.

This human constitution created by God is written in the hearts of all. It expresses essentially that no one should manipulate others or treat them as things, that no one should ambition to control the lives of God's people. To kill what God has made, or to do anything that would promote or abet the maiming of God's children must be avoided at all cost.

Regardless of my country of origin or my church affiliation, regardless of any pressure from civil authority to bear arms or of any blessing by ecclesiastical authority, I will never intentionally harm any of God's people. I desire wholeheartedly to use only peaceful means to attain peace and justice for all. Full of respect for God's Law and for people, I will not return violence for violence, or violate this law for any human, political or religious cause.

166. THE SECOND KIND OF HUMILITY

This kind is more demanding; it requires a greater degree of awareness and may require more reflection than the first. It means I neither seek, desire nor am I even inclined to have riches. It means that I have no preference for honor or dishonor, to have a long life rather than a short life. The one exception would be if either alternative would promote the service of God more clearly. Then a preference is laudable.

This spiritual attitude called "indifference" means that one's primary personal inclination is to serve God through helping people, rather than to seek praise, material things or even a longer life for oneself. It is based on a firm belief that God's presence flows in all people and in all things. It is an awareness that God's design is one of peace and compassion for all people. Indifference means that the truest human response is to serve God through people. This Second Kind of Humility offers such an experience of freedom and grace that a person feels that riches, honors and length of days are simply irrelevant. Clearly, the good of people and the service of God appear to be synonymous. God's love of mankind and neighborly love are seen as the obvious plan of creation.

In this second degree of humility there is an inherent disposition never to use people as means to an end, no matter how appealing, profitable or 'right', and never to interfere in the lives of others without their invitation.

Those who live by this degree of humility do not live under illusions, for they see all things illuminated by the light of Christ. There is a sense of non-obsessiveness. There is no righteousness or defensiveness about one's behavior. Society with its allurements, addictions, fears and fanaticism has no influence over this individual.

167. THE THIRD KIND OF HUMILITY

In the words of Ignatius, "This is the most perfect kind. It consists in this. If we suppose the first and second kind is attained, then whenever the praise and glory of God would be equally served, in order to imitate and be more like Christ, I desire and choose poverty with Christ poor rather than riches, and insults with Christ loaded with them rather than honors. I desire to be accounted as worthless and a fool for Christ, rather than to be esteemed as wise and prudent in this world. For this is how Christ was treated before me."

Can you imagine going through life without being bothered by competition or comparison, not being ambitious or greedy, not taking insults or offenses personally, not feeling embarrassed or self-conscious, not being worried about success, failure, acceptance or rejection? There would be so much time to contemplate, to enjoy, to serve, to love. There would be so much time for real life!

The desire to imitate Jesus' style of life involves seeing God in all things, especially in people. To see as Jesus saw means to respect life because it is God's creation and to appreciate God's special plan for each person. In order to become in reality more like Christ we need to understand the mind of Christ and desire to imitate His approach to the world. Among the people who knew Jesus personally some found his life-style inspiring, others found it disturbing. This Third Degree of Humility is not for everyone, though many might see the profound beauty in it.

Once we see Christ as thoroughly non-violent and patient, yet a revealer of society's deceptions, the style of Jesus becomes either appealing or disturbing. We see Jesus not just living carefully and constructively, but able to love the rejections and limitations of life as easily as another would accept possessions and praise. A loving acceptance and a Christlike indifference describes this Third Kind of Humility.

168. NOTE

"If one desires to attain this third kind of humility, it will help very much to use the three colloquies at the close of the meditation on the Three Classes of men (#156). He should beg our Lord to deign to choose him for this third kind of humility, which is higher and better, that he may the more imitate and serve him, provided equal or greater praise and service be given to the

Divine Majesty."

169. INTRODUCTION TO MAKING A CHOICE OF A WAY OF LIFE

In every good choice, as far as it depends on us, our intention must be direct. I must consider only the end for which I am created, that is, the praise of God our Lord and the salvation of my soul. Hence, whatever I choose must help me to this end. Awareness is the key.

I must not subject or fit the end to the means, but rather the means toward the end. The service of God is the end, my own long term good and the enhancement of people are the means. The care and service of God's people is the truest happiness; this is the kind of activity that provides the most lasting and most essential kind of joy. There are many signs to show that this service of God is not immediate or compulsive, or a verbal "Lord, Lord" or a superficial doing good, but rather a transparent and effective love for people.

When we are making choices, if we go directly to God and intend to serve God in these choices, we will find ourselves attracted by service and through serving to the beauty of God's plan of peace and joy for all His creatures. Service contains the greatest appeal, for it transcends the immediate satisfaction that our senses demand and fulfills a deeper human need. It is life-giving spiritually just as gratification of our various appetites gives biological satisfaction. The care of people fulfills a need that our heart has by nature. Responding to others is the clearest imitation of Christ and the deepest motivation for action.

The happiness of others adds to my happiness. There is a real and mysterious integration between the service of God and sharing with one another. God is True Happiness sharing Himself significantly with people through persons, graces, and events. People are happy when they are aware of God's Love for them, when they realize the Kingdom is for them, or when they truly take God's Love for granted in the fashion of children.

Therefore, my first aim should be to seek to serve God. After that, other intentions that are conducive may be made. If possible, nothing else ought to move me to use or to deprive myself of any of God's gifts except service, praise and enduring goodness.

MATTERS ABOUT WHICH
A CHOICE SHOULD BE MADE

170. FIRST POINT

It is necessary that all matters about which we wish to make a choice be either indifferent or good in themselves.

171. SECOND POINT

There are things that fall into the category of unchangeable choices or lifetime choices, and there are others that are choices for a period of time, as accepting or relinquishing a major appointment or opportunity. The first is long term and concerns a vocation for life, the latter is contingent upon places and things.

172. THIRD POINT

With regard to unchangeable life choices, if some previous choice had not been made with due order and if it was made with some inordinate attachments, then the realization of this and acceptance of this is valuable. We can understand that our actions will be performed with some side effects from this attachment, and the best we can do is to take care to live well in this particular life choice, and to do one's best in the situation in which there apparently can be no change.

There are many influences in our lives that would make it impossible to know fully the conditions and occasions that affected our decisions – how much of God's grace was present without our recognizing it and how much we were led by our upbringing and milieu. So we ought not to condemn our decisions from the past, but allow ourselves to see how God can work in and through all things, and lead us to the joy that He has promised.

173. FOURTH POINT

In matters that may be changed, if you have made a choice properly and with due order, without any yielding to the world's standards, there seems to be no reason why you should reconsider it. Just keep open to being creative and living up to your present potential in the choice you have made, so that there is a personal and creative response to life.

174. NOTE

If one notices that a choice had been made without sincerity and order and if one desires to bring forth fruit that is worthwhile and most pleasing in the sight of God, it will be profitable to remake this choice in the proper way. Ignatius is saying in effect, choose again – with understanding and wisdom, being more aware of the grace and enjoying the fruit.

175. THREE TIMES WHEN A CORRECT AND GOOD CHOICE OF A WAY OF LIFE MAY BE MADE

FIRST TIME

God moves you to act without hesitation and you feel without a shadow of a doubt that this is what you desire. The goodness in the action becomes one with your desire for it. There is an immediate chemical reaction between the senses and the inclination to act. The transparent quality of awareness is manifested. Desires are so strong and direct that choice and action appear as one. In modern jargon we say, "We are out of here," or "It is as good as done."

176. SECOND TIME

Understanding, like maturity, is derived through many experiences of desolation, consolation and the discernment of these diverse spirits. Besides the immediate awareness and clear choices as in the First Time, the Second is a process of working it through, discovering what a person wants to do and the choices a person has available. It evolves through weighing the relative values and examining the experiences that most deeply touch the heart. Time spent evaluating specifically what is least tasteful versus what is most refreshing can bring results as effective as in the First Time, since one's energy and attention have been thoroughly involved in formulating what the choice will be.

177. THIRD TIME

This is a time of tranquillity. One considers for what purpose man is created. With the desire to attain this, he then chooses as a means to this end a kind of life or state that will help him achieve this purpose. #23

It is a time when the soul experiences considerable freedom

and peace in the use of its natural powers and is not agitated by different spirits. In comparison with the second time where there is the experience of consolation and desolation, on this occasion the person is unpressured to make any decision. He is quite serene and objective as he prioritizes what he would like to do with his life.

Start at the beginning. What is the purpose of my life? Why was I created? What is this end for which I am created? Also inquire what is the purpose of the world - why did God create the world?

A typical tranquil time, hopefully, would be the time of retreat, when a person could be away, less pressured by worldly responsibilities. Examine the purpose of the world and your dreams; then select the best means for world peace and the best means to fulfill your dreams.

The greatest delight must be for a person to belong to a family or do work with a community that is serving others. This person needs to choose the particular vocation that will bring good news to others while providing the utmost satisfaction to himself.

178. TWO WAYS IN THE THIRD TIME

If a choice of a way of life has not been made in the First or Second Time, then use the following two ways for making a choice in times of tranquillity.

FIRST WAY

This contains six points.

FIRST POINT

This is to place before my mind the object with regard to which I wish to make a choice, or anything else that may be an object of a choice subject to change. Visualize the choice to be made as clearly as possible.

179. SECOND POINT

It is necessary to keep as my aim the end for which I am created, the desire to do God's will and the action of doing God's work. The end is directed toward a world of love and peace, and the means is similar, a heart of happiness and peace. If I can find happiness and peace, I will be in a credible position for passing on the Good News to others. My aim is trifold, God's will, a world at peace and my own happiness.

If I can feel indifferent, unattached and with no strong inordinate attachments, then I will not be unduly influenced by some hidden desires.

When I feel balanced and free I am able to look at many alternatives honestly and fairly. Ignatius called this "a balance at equilibrium." At this stage I am clearly ready to follow whatever I perceive is more for the glory of God, more for the end for which I am created.

180. THIRD POINT

I should beg for the grace to bring my mind and my will into harmony so that my choices and my actions are consistent. When I am doing what I desire and I am choosing what I think is most appropriate, there is no confusion.

I ask for the grace to be moved by a clear and direct attraction like the First Time #175, or for the grace to be moved as in the Second Time #176, where I would carefully weigh the experiences of consolation and desolation.

181. FOURTH POINT

This will be to weigh the matter by reckoning the number of advantages and benefits that would accrue to me if I had this particular office or object. I will also weigh the disadvantages and dangers that might be present if I accepted this position or thing.

182. FIFTH POINT

After I have pondered in this vein, I will consider which alternative appears more reasonable. When I come to a decision in the matter under deliberation it must be based on the values presented to my reason, rather than because of any sensual inclination.

183. SIXTH POINT

After such a choice or decision, the one who has made it must turn with great diligence to prayer and offer God the choice and see if there is any sense of acceptance and confirmation.

Will this decision further peace and harmony in the world? Is there a sense of consolation while this offering is presented?

This sixth point can reveal a sense of clarity similar to the transparency of the First Time where no hesitation or doubt is present.

184. SECOND WAY

This contains four rules and a note.

FIRST RULE

The attraction to do God's will and the inspiration to offer oneself for the service of others arises purely from the love of God. The clarity of intention, the means and the end are transparent.

185. SECOND RULE

Imagine you are introduced to someone you care for immediately and whom you would like to see sublimely happy. Picture this person with the same kind of quest as presented here and with the need to make a decision. Trying to be as objective as possible, and after asking pertinent questions, what would you tell this person to help him or her decide the best path for happiness?

Was your suggestion practical? How did you feel about it? Could you pursue the same process for yourself? How would your choice vary?

186. THIRD RULE

This rule and the next make use of projection as a help to be objective and subjective. Maybe this reflection would be less complicated, though more dramatic, if I imagine I were at the hour of my death. If I had to relive that decision would I have made the same choice? This reflection might provide just the perspective I need to help me make a decision. It may at least help me sort out my biases or reveal some doubts.

Do I still need to weigh the matter further?

187. FOURTH RULE

Let me imagine myself standing in the presence of Jesus, my affectionate Friend and Brother, at the end of my life. Reflect on what decision in the present matter under consideration I wish I had made. What would fill me with special happiness in the presence of Jesus? What choice now would give me the greatest consolation then? Once again I am looking for that which would bring the most joy as I relate with Jesus.

188. NOTE

Guided by the rules given above I will make my decision and offer it to God as directed in the Sixth Point, (#183). As I pray in the presence of God I make my offering and I look for acceptance, confirmation and clarity.

189. DIRECTIONS FOR THE AMENDMENT AND REFORMATION OF ONE'S WAY OF LIVING IN HIS STATE OF LIFE

Sometimes a person might not be able to make a choice because he is already into a state of life which cannot be changed. However, it is still worthwhile to propose a way for each person to renew his commitment and manner of living by setting before him the highest purpose for his life and his special role in giving glory to God.

We propose that he examines his home and work environment, his pattern of decision making, how he relates to others, and how he reflects the gentleness of Christ in word and example. He should consider what part of his means should be used for the support and welfare of his family and how much should be set aside for the poor.

Let him desire and seek nothing except the greater praise and glory of God as the aim of all he does. Everyone must keep in mind that his spiritual progress will be in proportion to his listening to his own deepest inspiration, and to the degree of his awareness and response to the graces that surround him.

Spiritual Exercises

THIRD WEEK

FIRST DAY

190. FIRST CONTEMPLATION
JESUS GOES FROM BETHANY
TO JERUSALEM

THE LAST SUPPER MATTHEW 26: 1 - 29 # 289
JOHN 13: 1 - 30 # 289

After three preludes there are six points and a colloquy.
Pray the usual preparatory prayer.

191. FIRST PRELUDE

Recall some of the details preceding the event, how Jesus carefully planned and spoke about this evening and then His final
meal. Spend some time picturing the events of the evening.

He said to his disciples, "In two day's time it will be the
Passover Festival, as you know, and the Son of Man will be handed over to be crucified."

On the first day of the Festival of Unleaven Bread the disciples
came to Jesus and asked him, "Where do you want us to make
the preparations for you to eat the Passover?" Go to a certain person in the city, and tell him: The Teacher says, "My hour has
come; my disciples and I will celebrate the Passover at your
house."

When evening came He was at table with the twelve disciples.
Now as they were eating, Jesus took some bread, and when He
had said the blessing He broke it and gave it to the disciples.
"Take and eat," He said, "This is my body." Then he took a cup,
and when he returned thanks he gave it to them. "Drink all of you
from this," He said, "for this is my blood, the blood of the
covenant, which is to be poured out for many for the forgiveness
of sins."

Jesus knew that the Father had put everything into his hands,
and that He had come from God and was returning to God. He
then poured water into a basin and began to wash the disciples'
feet and to wipe them with the towel he was wearing. Jesus said
to Simon Peter, "At the moment you do not know what I am
doing, but later you will understand."

If I, then, the Lord and Master, have washed your feet, you

should wash each other's feet. I have given you an example, so that you may copy what I have done to you. Now that you know this, happiness will be yours if you behave accordingly.

192. SECOND PRELUDE

Picture the way from Bethany to Jerusalem. Recall the description of the place of the Last Supper.

193. THIRD PRELUDE

I discover my heart's desire and then make a request for its fulfillment.

194. FIRST POINT

Jesus eats the Paschal Lamb with His disciples, to whom He predicts His death. I see the people at supper and reflect on my reaction and response.

SECOND POINT. He washes the feet of the disciples. Peter hesitates, "Lord do you wash my feet?" Jesus replies, "I have given you an example that as I have done you also must do. Listen to their conversation and seek to draw fruit from it.

THIRD POINT. He says, "This is my body. Take and eat." See what they are doing and seek to draw fruit from it.

195. FOURTH POINT

Consider the interior suffering Jesus endures and what he desires to accomplish with His self-offering. Strive to enter this experience with compassion.

196. FIFTH POINT

Consider the humility of Jesus in facing life and death, and His serenity and confidence as He confronts each event on the path to Calvary.

197. SIXTH POINT

What is my response to this salvific offering of Jesus?

198. COLLOQUY

Share your feelings and let Jesus reveal His own deep affection; then conclude the meditation with the Our Father.

199. NOTE

In the colloquy, one should talk over motives and present petitions according to circumstances. Thus he may be tempted or he may enjoy consolation, he may desire this virtue or he may want to dispose himself in this particular way, or he may seek to grieve or rejoice according to the matter that he is contemplating. Finally, he should ask what he more earnestly desires with regard to some particular interests.

200. SECOND CONTEMPLATION
THE LAST SUPPER
TO THE AGONY IN THE GARDEN
MATTHEW 26: 30 - 46; MARK 14: 32 - 44 # 290
Pray the usual preparatory prayer.

201. FIRST PRELUDE

This is the history of the mystery. Jesus crossed the Kedron Valley with the eleven disciples and came to a small estate called Gethsemane. Eight of the disciples were left at a place in the valley, and the other three in a part of the garden. Then Jesus began His prayer, and His sweat became as drops of blood. Three times He prayed to His Father and went to rouse His disciples from sleep.

When the men sent by the priests, elders and scribes came looking for Jesus, they fell to the ground when Jesus said, "I am He." After Judas' identifying kiss (they did not know Jesus, the man or His message), and after Peter had cut off the ear of Malchus, Jesus was seized as a malefactor. He was led down through the valley and again up the slope to the house of Annas.

202. SECOND PRELUDE

This is to see the place. It will be here to consider the Mount of Olives, the valley, likewise the garden, its breadth, length, and appearance.

203. THIRD PRELUDE

This is to ask for what I desire. In the Passion it is proper to ask for sorrow with Christ in sorrow, anguish with Christ in anguish, tears and deep grief because of the great affliction Jesus endures.
FIRST POINT. When the Supper was finished, Jesus, goes forth with His disciples to Mt. Olivet. He left them in

Gethsemane, saying, "Sit you here whilst I go yonder and pray."

SECOND POINT. Accompanied by Peter, James and John, He prays three times to the Father, saying, "My Father, if it be possible let this cup pass from me, yet not as I will." And falling into an agony He prayed the more earnestly.

THIRD POINT. Jesus is overwhelmed, "My soul is sorrowful unto death."

204. NOTE I

In this second contemplation, after the preparatory prayer and the three preludes given above, the same way of proceeding in the points and colloquies is to be observed as was followed in the first contemplation.

The two Repetitions and the Application of the Senses should be made on the subject matter of the two contemplations. The preparatory prayer and the preludes adapted to the subject of the exercise are always to precede. The form to be observed is the same as that given and explained in the Second Week. # 101

205. NOTE II

As far as age, health, and physical constitution permit, the exercitant will perform five exercises each day, or fewer.

206. NOTE III

In the Third Week some modification of the second and sixth Additional Directions is necessary. # 74 & # 76

The second will be that as soon as I awake I will call to mind where I am going and the purpose. I will briefly summarize the contemplation on which I am about to enter. I will make an effort while rising and dressing to be aware of the subject matter I am considering and mentally stay present to it.

The sixth Additional Direction will be changed as follows. I will take care not to bring up pleasing thoughts, even though they are good and holy. Rather I will rouse myself to sorrow realizing the gravity of Jesus' suffering especially during the week of His Passion.

207. NOTE IV

The Particular Examination of Conscience should be made on the Exercises and the Additional Directions as applied to this Week, as was done in the past Week.

208. FIRST CONTEMPLATION
FROM THE AGONY TO ANNAS' HOUSE

MATTHEW 26: 47 - 58; LUKE 22: 47 - 57;
MARK 14: 44 - 68 # 291

FIRST POINT. Our Lord allows Himself to be kissed by Judas, and to be seized as a robber. He says to them, "Have you come as against a robber with swords and clubs to arrest me? Day after day I sat in the temple teaching and you seized me not."

SECOND POINT. Peter wounds the servant of the High Priest. Jesus says to him, "Put your sword back, for all who draw the sword will die by the sword."

THIRD POINT. Deserted by His disciples, He is led to Annas. Peter who had stayed outside the High Priest's Palace denied he was a disciple. The High Priest questioned Jesus about His teaching. Jesus answered, "I have spoken openly for the world to hear." Christ was struck in the face and asked, "Is that the way to answer the High Priest?"

SECOND CONTEMPLATION
FROM ANNAS TO THE HOUSE OF CAIPHAS

MATTHEW 26: 57 - 68; MARK 14: 53 - 72;
LUKE 22: 63 - 71 # 292

FIRST POINT. Near the house of Caiphas, Peter denied Him twice. When our Lord looked upon him, he went out and wept bitterly.

SECOND POINT. Jesus remained bound the whole night.

THIRD POINT. Those who kept Him bound buffeted Him, blasphemed Him and covered His face and struck Him with the palms of their hands and asked Him, "Prophesy who was it that struck Thee."

There will be Two Repetitions and the Application of the Senses (as explained in # 62 and # 118).

THIRD DAY

FIRST CONTEMPLATION
FROM CAIPHAS TO PILATE'S HOUSE

MATTHEW 27: 1 - 26; LUKE 23: 1 - 7; MARK 15: 1 - 15 # 293

FIRST POINT. The chief priests, elders and scribes had Jesus bound and took Him away and handed Him over to Pilate, and accused Him before the governor, saying, "We have found this man inciting our people to revolt, opposing the payment of tribute to Caesar, and claiming to be Christ, a king."

SECOND POINT. After Pilate had examined Him several times, he said, "I find no case against this man."

THIRD POINT. Barabbas, the robber, was preferred to Him, "The chief priests shouted, "Not this man but Barabbas."

SECOND CONTEMPLATION
FROM PILATE TO HEROD

LUKE 23: 6 - 12 # 294

FIRST POINT. Pilate sent Jesus, the Galilean, to Herod the Tetrarch of Galiee.

SECOND POINT. Herod curiously asked many questions, and Jesus answered nothing, though the scribes and priests accused Him constantly.

THIRD POINT. Herod puts a white garment on him - the color for a fool.

There will be Two Repetitions and the Application of the Senses as explained.

FOURTH DAY

FIRST CONTEMPLATION
FROM HEROD TO PILATE

LUKE 23: 13 - 25; MATTHEW 27: 1 - 31 # 295

FIRST POINT. Herod sent Jesus back to Pilate, and because of this they became friends, though before they were enemies.

SECOND POINT. Pilate took Jesus and had Him scourged, and the soldiers made a crown of thorns and placed it on His head. They put a purple cloak about Him, and came to Him and said, "Hail king of the Jews." And they gave Him blows.

THIRD POINT. Pilate led Jesus before the people, "Behold your Man!" The chief priests yelled repeatedly, "Crucify him!"

SECOND CONTEMPLATION - Use these other versions of the same scripture referring to Jesus before Herod and Pilate. MARK 15: 13 - 25; JOHN 19: 1 - 16 # 295

Use Two Repetitions and the Application of the Senses with these contemplations.

FIFTH DAY

FIRST CONTEMPLATION
FROM PILATE'S HOUSE
TO THE CRUCIFIXION
MARK 15: 21 - 39; JOHN 19: 13 - 37 # 296

FIRST POINT. After the chief priests said, "We have no king but Caesar," Pilate delivered up Jesus to be crucified.

SECOND POINT. He carried the cross upon His shoulders and when He was no longer able Simon of Cyrene carried it for Him.

THIRD POINT. They crucified Him between two thieves. Above the cross was a sign in three languages, Jesus of Nazareth, King of the Jews.

SECOND CONTEMPLATION
FROM THE CROSS UP TO HIS DEATH
JOHN 19: 23 - 37; MATTHEW 27: 35 - 52;
MARK 15: 24 - 38; LUKE 23: 34 - 46 # 297

FIRST POINT. He spoke seven words upon the cross: 1) He prayed for those who crucified Him. 2) He pardoned the thief. 3) He recommended John to His Mother. 4) He begged with a loud voice, "I thirst." 5) He cried, "Why have you forsaken me?" 6) He gasped, "It is consummated." 7) He prayed, "Father, into thy hands I commend my spirit."

SECOND POINT. The sun was darkened and the veil of the Temple was torn from top to bottom.

THIRD POINT. They blasphemed Him saying, "Come down from the cross." His garments were divided and His side was pierced with a lance.

Use Two Repetitions and the Application of the Senses.

SIXTH DAY

FIRST CONTEMPLATION
FROM THE CROSS TO THE SEPULCHRE
LUKE 23: 44 - 56; MATTHEW 27: 51 - 66 # 298

FIRST POINT. Joseph of Arimathea went to Pilate and asked for the body of Jesus. Joseph took the body wrapped it in a clean shroud and put it in his own new tomb.

SECOND POINT. The chief priests and the Pharisees went to

Pilate and said, "Your excellency, we recall that this imposter said while he was still alive, that after three days he would rise again. Give the order to have the sepulchre kept secure until the third day."

THIRD POINT. "You may have your guard," said Pilate to the chief priests.

SECOND CONTEMPLATION
FROM THE BURIAL TO
OUR LADY'S HOUSE

JOHN 19: 31 - 42; MARK 15: 37 - 47

Use Two Repetitions and the Application of the Senses.

SEVENTH DAY

FIRST CONTEMPLATION
THE WHOLE PASSION

MATTHEW 26 & 27; MARK 14 & 15

SECOND CONTEMPLATION
THE WHOLE PASSION

LUKE 22 & 23; JOHN 18 & 19

In place of the two Repetitions and the Application of the Senses, one should consider as frequently as possible throughout this whole day the Body of Christ. Ponder also the reverent anointing and manner of the burial. Consider likewise, the desolation of our Lady, her great sorrow and weariness, and also that of the disciples.

209. NOTE

If one wishes to spend more time on the passion, he should meditate on the Last Supper; second, on the washing of feet; third, the institution of the Eucharist; fourth, Christ's parting address, and so on for the other contemplations and mysteries.

In like manner, after the passion is finished, he may devote one whole day to the consideration of the first half of the passion, and a second day to the other half, and a third day to the passion as a whole.

On the other hand, if he should wish to spend less time on the passion, he may meditate on the Last Supper at evening prayer, the Agony in the Garden in the morning; Jesus before Annas for the next meditation and Jesus before Caiphas for the fourth meditation; and instead of the Application of the Senses, consider Jesus before Pilate for the final prayer period.

In this way, without repetitions or Applications of the Senses, there should be five exercises each day, using a distinct mystery of the life of Christ for each meditation. After he has finished the whole passion in this way, he may use another day to go through the entire passion, either in one exercise or in several, as is deemed best for his greater profit.

RULES WITH REGARD TO EATING

It is interesting that Ignatius positioned these rules for eating between the Third and Fourth Week of the Exercises. He obviously assumed a greater freedom on the part of the retreatant, and rightly so, and expected the retreatant to have a clear understanding and a mature interpretation of the rules that follow.

Mealtimes during retreat ought to provide not just nourishment for the body and a regular break from the day's exercises but must also foster the spirit of the day's reflections. To stay in shape requires not just care in performing the assigned exercises but consistent vigilance with regard to quality and quantity of intake.

And so to secure for the future due order in the use of food the following basic rules should prove helpful.

210. FIRST RULE

There is less need of abstinence from bread and vegetables, since they are not foods concerning which the appetite is wont to be so inordinate as with other kinds of foods, rich in sugar, proteins, calories and fat.

211. SECOND RULE

With regard to liquid refreshment, one should consider carefully what would be helpful, and what would be harmful especially with regard to wine, caffeineted or alcoholic beverages.

212. THIRD RULE

To avoid disorder concerning foods, abstinence may be practiced in two ways:

First, by accustoming oneself to eat coarser foods like grains, greens and vegetables and consciously choosing health foods and healthy foods as a matter of course.

Second, if and when delicacies are taken, to deliberately eat them sparingly.

213. FOURTH RULE

During retreat simple and basic nourishment should be the food of preference, that which is satisfying and also the least distracting from the task at hand. To partake of proper and adequate sustenance for the body is essential as it prevents obsession with food outside of meal times. 3-0-1 is an excellent program to follow: 3) three meals a day, 0) nothing between meals, and 1) one day at a time.

Outside of retreat, eating habits like other habits are quite unconscious and automatic behaviors. Whereas, on retreat the senses are especially aware of taste and other bodily sensations, habitual or otherwise.

Through sensitivity and awareness, discover what portions are suitable for each meal so that the various Spiritual Exercises are performed with energy and enthusiasm.

214. FIFTH RULE

Until there is ease with one's diet, be attentive as when an athlete is preparing for a race. Initially, he is extremely concerned about his diet. On one hand he wants to be energetic and feel fit and so is careful to eat properly. On the other, he eats not just to satisfy his hunger, but he has the athletic contest in mind.

215. SIXTH RULE

It is a special grace to taste and appreciate food in its variety of flavors and distinctive tastes, especially when it is freshly prepared. To derive full benefit from the experience of a meal, it is best shared with companions of choice. Recall how frequently Jesus would be working or praying and then stop to share a simple yet memorable meal with his friends. When friends are not available or while eating alone, it is refreshing to be surrounded by natural scenery to give your thoughts a rest and to enjoy a new perspective. A third alternative is have a book, magazine or newspaper available, so that the mind can have its own relaxation while the body's energy is being restored.

216. SEVENTH RULE

As the retreatant prepares and plans the meditations for each day with the director, so meals should be an integral part of the preparation. While the refectory or dining room may be the typical and traditional location for most meals, think creatively about outdoor locations, other sites, a change of scenery, a boxed lunch at some distance from the residence, a meal by the shore, in the hills, by a lake. With fresh air, open mindedness and a taste of personal freedom the heart is renewed. Memorable meals are powerful prayers and are invaluable helps to the subsequent exercises.

217. EIGHTH RULE

If any disorder or uneasiness is detected with regard to meals themselves or food consumption, it will be helpful either after eating or when one has no particular desire for food to reflect on the actual problem and decide firmly about the next meal.

Since eating is a daily necessity, it should be in conformity with your will and desire. Any inordinate appetite can affect one's prayer in particular and life in general, and needs to be mastered. To be free means not to be at the mercy of anyone or anything, this includes food.

Spiritual Exercises

FOURTH WEEK

FIRST DAY

218. THE RESURRECTION AND REUNION WITH HIS FATHER

LUKE 15: 20, 22 - 24

Pray the usual preparatory prayer.

FIRST POINT. "He arose and came to His Father."

SECOND POINT. "While he was yet at a distance, His Father saw him and had compassion, embraced him and kissed him."

THIRD POINT. "Bring the best robe... for My Son was dead and is alive again." And they began to celebrate.

THE FIRST APPARITION TO HIS MOTHER # 299

Though this is not mentioned explicitly in the Scripture it must be considered as stated. For Scripture assumes the obvious, as it is written, "Are you also without understanding?"

Pray the usual preparatory prayer.

219. FIRST PRELUDE

This is the history. After Christ expired on the cross and was buried, on the third day He appears to His Mother.

220. SECOND PRELUDE

This is a mental representation of the place. Here it will be to see the setting of the holy sepulchre and the arrangement of rooms in Mary's house.

221. THIRD PRELUDE

This will be to ask for what I desire. Here it will be to ask for the grace to be glad and rejoice intensely because of the great joy and the glory of Christ our Lord.

222. FIRST POINT

Jesus came and comforted His Mother. See this reunion at Mary's house.

SECOND POINT. Listen to their conversation.

THIRD POINT. Watch what they are doing.

223. FOURTH POINT

This will be to consider the divinity, which seemed to hide itself during the passion, now appearing and manifesting itself so miraculously.

224. FIFTH POINT

Consider the office of consoler that Christ our Lord exercises, and compare it with the way in which friends are wont to console each other.

225. COLLOQUY

Close with a colloquy, or colloquies, as the circumstances suggest, and at the end say the Our Father.

226. NOTE I

In the subsequent contemplations, all the mysteries from the Resurrection to the Ascension inclusive are to be gone through in the manner indicated below.

The contemplation on the apparition to Mary, given above, will serve as a guide. The preludes will be the same, but adapted to the matter being considered. The five points will be the same. The Additional Directions will be as given below. In all the rest, for example, with regard to the Repetitions (# 118), the Application of the Senses (# 121), the shortening or lengthening of the mysteries, etc., the Week devoted to the passion may serve as a model.

227. NOTE II

Ordinarily, it is more in keeping with this Week than with those that have passed to have four exercises a day instead of five.

The first contemplation will be on rising in the morning, the second before the afternoon meal, the third in the afternoon will be the repetition. The fourth meditation in the evening will be the Application of the Senses regarding the matter of the two contemplations of the day.

In making the Application of the Senses, attention and more time is to be given to the more important points where you were more deeply moved and where spiritual relish was greater.

228. NOTE III

Regarding the preparation for each meditation, though in all the contemplations a definite number of points is given, say three or five, the one who is contemplating may make use of more or fewer as seems better for him. For this reason it will be very useful before entering on the contemplation to foresee and determine a definite number of points that are to be used.

229. NOTE IV

In the Fourth Week a change is to be made in the second (# 74), sixth (# 78), seventh (# 79) and tenth (# 82 - 85) Additional Directions.

The second will be, as soon as I awake, to place before my mind the contemplation I am to enter upon, and then to strive to feel joy and happiness at the great joy and happiness of Christ our Lord.

The sixth will be to call to mind thoughts that cause pleasure, happiness, and spiritual joy.

The seventh will be to make use of the light and the pleasures of the seasons, for example, the warmth of the sun in summer or the refreshing coolness of winter and the sanctuary of the fireplace if it will help the retreatant to rejoice with the Creator and Redeemer.

The tenth will be to take more delight during and after mealtimes though always with temperance and moderation.

THE SECOND APPARITION
TO MARY MAGDALENE
MARK 16: 1 - 11 # 300

FIRST PRELUDE. This is the history.

SECOND PRELUDE. This is a mental representation of the place.

THIRD PRELUDE. This will be to ask for what I desire. Here it will be to ask for the grace to be glad and rejoice intensely because of the great joy and the glory of Christ our Lord.

FIRST POINT. Very early in the morning Mary Magdalene, Mary the mother of James, and Salome go to the tomb. They say to one another, "Who will roll away the stone for us from the entrance of the tomb?"

SECOND POINT. They see the stone had already been rolled

back. And a young man in a white robe said to them, "Jesus of Nazareth, who was crucified, has risen, he is not here."

THIRD POINT. He appeared to Mary of Magdala. When Jesus said, "Mary" she understood.

COLLOQUY. Close with a colloquy or colloquies, as the circumstances suggest, and at the end say the Our Father.

One Repetition and the Application of the Senses should be made on the subject matter of the two contemplations.

SECOND DAY

THE THIRD APPARITION
TO THE TWO MARYS

MATTHEW 28: 1 - 10 # 301

FIRST PRELUDE. This is the history.

SECOND PRELUDE. This is a mental representation of the place.

THIRD PRELUDE. This will be to ask for what I desire. Here it will be to ask for the grace to be glad and rejoice intensely because of the great joy and the glory of Christ our Lord.

FIRST POINT. The two Marys ran from the empty tomb filled with awe and great joy to tell the disciples what they had seen.

SECOND POINT. Jesus greets them on the way. They fell down and clasped His feet.

THIRD POINT. Jesus says to them, "Fear not! Go tell my brothers that they must leave for Galilee. They will see me there."

COLLOQUY. Close with a colloquy or colloquies, as the circumstances suggest, and at the end say the Our Father.

THE FOURTH APPARITION
TO PETER

LUKE 24: 9 - 12, 33 - 34 # 302

FIRST PRELUDE. This is the history.

SECOND PRELUDE. This is a mental representation of the place.

THIRD PRELUDE. This will be to ask for what I desire. Here it will be to ask for the grace to be glad and rejoice intensely because of the great joy and the glory of Christ our Lord.

FIRST POINT. When Peter heard from the women, he went with haste to the tomb.

SECOND POINT. He entered the tomb and saw the empty

linens but nothing else.

THIRD POINT. While Peter was reflecting on what he was told and what he had seen, Jesus appeared to him.

COLLOQUY. Close with a colloquy or colloquies, as the circumstances suggest, and at the end say the Our Father.

One Repetition and the Application of the Senses should be made on the subject matter of the two contemplations.

THIRD DAY

THE FIFTH APPARITION
ON THE ROAD TO EMMAUS

LUKE 24: 13 - 35 # 303

FIRST PRELUDE. This is the history.

SECOND PRELUDE. This is a mental representation of the place.

THIRD PRELUDE. This will be to ask for what I desire. Here it will be to ask for the grace to be glad and rejoice intensely because of the great joy and the glory of Christ our Lord.

FIRST POINT. While two disciples were going to Emmaus Jesus came up and walked by their side.

SECOND POINT. He reprehends them, showing them by the Scriptures that Christ must die and rise again. "You foolish men, so slow to believe the full message of the prophets!"

THIRD POINT. While he was at table with them, He took the bread, said the blessing, broke it and handed it to them. And their eyes were opened and they recognized Him.

COLLOQUY. Close with a colloquy or colloquies, as the circumstances suggest, and at the end say the Our Father.

THE SIXTH APPARITION
TO THE DISCIPLES

JOHN 20: 19 - 25 # 304

FIRST PRELUDE. This is the history.

SECOND PRELUDE. This is a mental representation of the place.

THIRD PRELUDE. This will be to ask for what I desire. Here it will be to ask for the grace to be glad and rejoice intensely because of the great joy and the glory of Christ our Lord.

FIRST POINT. On the first day of the week the disciples were gathered together for fear of the Chief Priests.

SECOND POINT. Jesus came and stood among them and said, "Peace be with you." And He showed them His hands and His side.

THIRD POINT. Jesus said to them, "As the Father sent me, so am I sending you."

COLLOQUY. Close with a colloquy or colloquies, as the circumstances suggest, and at the end say the Our Father.

One Repetition and the Application of the Senses should be made on the subject matter of the two contemplations.

FOURTH DAY

THE SEVENTH APPARITION
TO THOMAS

JOHN 20: 24 - 29 # 305

FIRST PRELUDE. This is the history.

SECOND PRELUDE. This is a mental representation of the place.

THIRD PRELUDE. This will be to ask for what I desire. Here it will be to ask for the grace to be glad and rejoice intensely because of the great joy and the glory of Christ our Lord.

FIRST POINT. Thomas had not been present on the previous occasions and he could not believe.

SECOND POINT. Eight days later, Jesus came in and said to Thomas, "Put your finger here, and give my your hand and put it in my side."

THIRD POINT. Thomas answered, "My Lord and my God."

COLLOQUY. Close with a colloquy or colloquies, as the circumstances suggest, and at the end say the Our Father.

THE EIGHTH APPARITION
TO SEVEN DISCIPLES

JOHN 21: 1 - 17 # 306

FIRST PRELUDE. This is the history.

SECOND PRELUDE. This is a mental representation of the place.

THIRD PRELUDE. This will be to ask for what I desire. Here it will be to ask for the grace to be glad and rejoice intensely because of the great joy and the glory of Christ our Lord.

FIRST POINT. Jesus appeared to seven who were having no success fishing. Then casting the net where He commanded, they were not able to haul in the quantity of fish.

SECOND POINT. John recognized Jesus on the shore and said, "It is the Lord." Peter jumped into the water.

THIRD POINT. Jesus provided breakfast, asked Peter three times, "Do you love me?" and then told Peter, "Feed my sheep."

COLLOQUY. Close with a colloquy or colloquies, as the circumstances suggest, and at the end say the Our Father.

One Repetition and the Application of the Senses should be made on the subject matter of the two contemplations.

FIFTH DAY

THE NINTH APPARITION
ON MT. TABOR

MATTHEW 28: 16 - 20 # 307

FIRST PRELUDE. This is the history.

SECOND PRELUDE. This is a mental representation of the place.

THIRD PRELUDE. This will be to ask for what I desire. Here it will be to ask for the grace to be glad and rejoice intensely because of the great joy and the glory of Christ our Lord.

FIRST POINT. Jesus had promised to meet the disciples on Mt. Tabor in Galilee.

SECOND POINT. Christ appears to them and says, "All authority in heaven and on earth is given to me."

THIRD POINT. "Go make disciples of all nations, teach them to observe all that I have commanded you; and know that I am with you always, yes, to the end of time."

COLLOQUY. Close with a colloquy or colloquies, as the circumstances suggest, and at the end say the Our Father.

THE TENTH APPARITION
TO THE FIVE HUNDRED

I CORINTHIANS 15: 6 # 308

SIXTH DAY

THE ELEVENTH APPARITION
TO JAMES
I CORINTHIANS 15: 7 # 309

THE TWELFTH APPARITION
TO JOSEPH OF ARIMATHEA
 # 310

THE SEVENTH DAY

THE THIRTEENTH APPARITION
TO PAUL
I CORINTHIANS 15: 8 # 311

FIRST PRELUDE. This is the history.

SECOND PRELUDE. This is a mental representation of the place.

THIRD PRELUDE. This will be to ask for what I desire. Here it will be to ask for the grace to be glad and rejoice intensely because of the great joy and the glory of Christ our Lord.

FIRST POINT. He appeared to Paul after His Ascension, "Last of all as to one born out of due time, He appeared to me."

SECOND POINT. He appeared to those who had gone before Him.

THIRD POINT. He appeared many times to His disciples and conversed with them.

COLLOQUY. Close with a colloquy or colloquies, as the circumstances suggest, and at the end say the Our Father.

THE ASCENSION OF CHRIST
OUR LORD
ACTS 1: 1 - 12 # 312

FIRST PRELUDE. This is the history.

SECOND PRELUDE. This is a mental representation of the place.

THIRD PRELUDE. This will be to ask for what I desire. Here it will be to ask for the grace to be glad and rejoice intensely because of the great joy and the glory of Christ our Lord.

FIRST POINT. Jesus manifested Himself for forty days to the

Apostles and had given them many proofs and worked many miracles. He spoke to them of the Kingdom of God and then commanded them to await in Jerusalem the promise of the Holy Spirit.

SECOND POINT. He led them to Mt. Olivet and He was lifted up before their eyes. And a cloud received Him out of their sight.

THIRD POINT. They were still staring into the sky when suddenly two men in white were standing near them who said, "Men of Galilee, why are you standing here looking into the sky? Jesus who has been taken up from you into heaven will come back in the same manner as you have seen Him go there."

COLLOQUY. Close with a colloquy or colloquies, as the circumstances suggest, and at the end say the Our Father.

One Repetition and the Application of the Senses should be made on the subject matter of the two contemplations.

PENTECOST

ACTS 2: 1 - 36; JOHN 20: 19 - 23

FIRST PRELUDE. This is the history.

SECOND PRELUDE. This is a mental representation of the place.

THIRD PRELUDE. This will be to ask for what I desire. Here it will be to ask for the grace to be glad and rejoice intensely because of the great joy and the glory of Christ our Lord.

FIRST POINT. When Pentecost day came they all met in one room. They heard what sounded like a powerful wind and then something appeared that seemed like tongues of fire.

SECOND POINT. They were all filled with the Holy Spirit and began speaking in foreign languages.

THIRD POINT. Peter stood up and addressed them. "All of us are witnesses to Jesus now raised to the height by God's right hand. And what you see and hear is the outpouring of that Spirit."

230. CONTEMPLATION TO ATTAIN LOVE OF GOD

FIRST

Love manifests itself in deeds as well as in words.

231. SECOND

Love consists in a mutual sharing of goods. For example, the lover gives and shares with the beloved what he possesses, or something that he is able to give. And vice versa, the beloved shares with the lover. Hence, if one has knowledge, honors or wealth he shares it with the one who does not possess it. Thus one always gives to the other.

PRAYER. The usual prayer.

232. FIRST PRELUDE

This is the representation of the place, which here is to behold myself standing in the presence of God our Lord and of His angels and saints, who intercede for me.

233. SECOND PRELUDE

This is to ask for what I desire. Here it will be to ask for an intimate knowledge of the wealth of blessings I have received, that filled with gratitude, I may love and serve in return.

234. FIRST POINT

This is to recall to mind the blessings of creation and redemption, and other significant favors I have received.

I will ponder the great affection God has for me, and how much He has given me, and finally, how much the Lord desires to give Himself to me according to His divine plan.

Then I will reflect upon myself, and consider, according to all reason and justice, what I ought to offer in return, that is, all I possess and myself with it. Then, moved by great feeling, I will make this offering of myself, referred to as the "Suscipe".

TAKE, LORD, AND RECEIVE

*TAKE, LORD AND RECEIVE ALL MY LIBER-
TY, MY MEMORY, MY UNDERSTANDING AND
MY ENTIRE WILL, ALL THAT I HAVE AND
POSSESS. THOU HAST GIVEN ALL TO ME.
TO THEE, O LORD I RETURN IT. ALL IS
THINE; DISPOSE OF IT WHOLLY ACCORD-
ING TO THY WILL. GIVE ME THY LOVE AND
THY GRACE, FOR THIS IS SUFFICIENT FOR
ME.*

235. SECOND POINT

This is to reflect how God dwells in creatures: in the elements giving them existence, in the plants given them life, in the animals conferring upon them sensation, in man bestowing understanding. So He dwells in me and gives me being, life, sensation, intelligence, and makes a temple of me, since I am created in the likeness and image of the Divine Majesty.

Then I will reflect upon myself again in the manner stated in the first point, or in some other way that may seem better.

The same should be observed with regard to each of the points given below.

236. THIRD POINT

This is to consider how God works for me in all creatures upon the face of the earth, that is, He conducts Himself as one who labors. Thus, in the heavens, the elements, the plants, the fruits, the cattle, etc., He gives being, conserves them, confers life and sensation, etc.

Then I will reflect on myself.

237. FOURTH POINT

This is to consider all blessings and gifts as descending from above. Thus, my limited power comes from the supreme and infinite power above, and so too, goodness and mercy descend from above as the rays of light descend from the sun, and as the waters flow from the mountains.

Then I will reflect on myself, as has been said.

Conclude with a colloquy and the Our Father.

238. THREE METHODS OF PRAYER

Prayer may be described as directing your mind, your intentions and your heart's desires toward spiritual concerns. It affects your thoughts, it occupies the mind, it includes the focus of your attention on a particular matter. The body is certainly involved and so the overall emotional health and physical well being of the person is of great influence on the type of prayer recommended. And so the typical and current needs of the individual will affect the whole tenor and approach to prayer.

While we do refer to inspired words, or scripture passages as prayer. The words in themselves are not prayer. Prayer is the activity of people who recognize the presence of God in their lives and who respond to that presence. And while a set formula of words may be the actual starting points, what occurs during the reflection period is the actual prayer.

Ignatius took into account all the basic styles of prayer in his listing of three methods: Meditative Prayer - careful consideration of a truth, or a series of truths; Contemplative Prayer - pondering one word or idea; Mystical Prayer - giving attention to each moment - one breath at a time.

THE FIRST METHOD OF PRAYER

The first method describes using your intellect to examine the great truths of history, in particular the commandments and how they are written in the hearts of all people of good will. Then apply this method to the basic propensities in people to overdo things, the capital sins. Ignatius recommends that the three powers of the soul and the five senses of the body get equal consideration.

These meditations are not so much a literal method of praying but rather a way of proceeding that offer such marvelous insights that often the immediate result is that the mind and heart are raised to God in prayer. When one meditates on truth and searches for the truth, God is found.

ON THE TEN COMMANDMENTS

What better starting point for prayer than the summary of loving God and loving neighbor as indicated by the Decalogue. *EXODUS 20.*

239. ADDITIONAL DIRECTION

As in the Second Week, before entering the prayer period, while walking or seated, recollect the purpose of this particular exercise and what points I will consider. # 130

240. PRAYER

I will ask for a clearer understanding of each of the Commandments so as to observe them better and glorify the Lord more. A preparatory prayer should be made, for example, I ask God for the grace to know how I may have failed in the observance of any of the commandments. I might also ask for the grace to help me to make amends as necessary.

241. METHOD

Consider and think over one commandment at a time, asking myself how I have observed it and in what manner I have failed. Spending about five minutes reflecting on each commandment, for each one where I find fault, I will ask for forgiveness and say the Our Father.

242. NOTE I

It is not necessary to delay on areas where there in no confusion and no problem. Where there is doubt or difficulty, devote more time to the examination and application of that particular Commandment until clarity is achieved. This same approach should be applied to the meditation on the capital sins.

243. NOTE II

At the close of each meditation, after requesting the grace to lead a holier life, end with a colloquy.

ON THE CAPITAL SINS

This same method is to be applied to the truth of our own personality. Pondering the capacity and propensity for misusing our inherent compulsions leads to realism about our own limitations. The label of the seven capital sins provides an order for our reflection.

244. METHOD

Using the Additional Direction # 239 and the preparatory

prayer # 240, follow the same procedure considering one sin at a time. However, while considering the Commandments the object was observance, with the capital sins it is avoidance.

245. NOTE

For greater understanding of the faults committed under the umbrella of capital sins a positive approach would be to consider the contrary virtues. One should then resolve to endeavor by devout exercises to acquire and retain the seven virtues.

ON THE THREE POWERS OF THE SOUL

The Insights into our own God-given power to think and feel and choose are the themes of the third consideration. To know one's strengths and weaknesses in processing ideas and emotions is essential to be a disciple of Christ. To be sensitive to one's personal pattern for making choices and to become more conscious of the typical distractions make life worth living.

246. METHOD

With regard to the three powers of the soul, observe the same method, measure of time, and additional direction as for the Commandments. As usual, begin with a preparatory prayer and close with a colloquy.

ON THE FIVE SENSES OF THE BODY

The meditation on our five senses provides a tangible source for finding God in all things. These are the filters of the soul; these senses are our contact with the world. They are remarkable gifts that are worth a lifetime of gratitude and deserve reverent care in their use. To pray with each one can bring helpful revelations and lasting rewards.

247. METHOD

Follow the same method as described above.

248. NOTE

In the preparatory prayer for the subject matter regarding the use of the senses, it will be beneficial to request for the grace to imitate Christ in each instance. After the consideration end with the Our Father.

If one wishes to imitate Mary in the use of her senses, let the preparatory prayer be directed to Our Lady and after the consideration, close with a Hail Mary.

249. THE SECOND METHOD OF PRAYER
This consists in contemplating the meaning of each word of a prayer.

250. ADDITIONAL DIRECTION
Before beginning this meditation focus for a few minutes on the purpose of this prayer period and the goals and means you will use. # 239

251. PREPARATORY PRAYER
Choose to whom you will address this prayer
METHOD. The mind is quieter during this prayer. One may kneel or sit whichever is more conducive to devotion. He should keep his eyes closed, or focused in one direction. Then let him say, "Father" and continue meditating on this word as long as he finds consolation. Discovering new meanings, comparisons and personal references to this same word will be sources of consolation as well. Continue with the next word of the Our Father or with any other prayer which one wishes to use.

253. RULE I
He should use this way of praying for the entire hour, and then end with the recitation of one of the following: the Creed, the Hail Mary, Soul of Christ or the Hail Holy Queen.

254. RULE II
If the retreatant finds abundant matter for thought and much consolation in just one or two words, he should not be anxious to proceed, though the whole hour be taken up with what he has found. When the hour is over, let him say the rest of the prayer as the concluding prayer.

255. RULE III
If the retreatant has been occupied with one or two words for the entire hour, when he wishes to pray at another time let him commence with the words that immediately follow those two.

256. NOTE I

After praying this method using the Our Father and the Hail Mary, the retreatant should choose other forms of prayer.

257. NOTE II

At the end of the prayer, he should turn to the person to whom the prayer is directed, and in a few words ask for the graces which he needs most.

258. THIRD METHOD OF PRAYER

How shall we title this simple method of prayer? The prayer of unity; The prayer of the Spirit; The prayer of creation; The prayer of breathing; The prayer of life? God's spirit hovered over the water. GENESIS 1: 2 Jesus breathed on them and said, "Receive the Holy Spirit." JOHN 20: 22 Ignatius discovered the power, the wonder and the presence of prayer in each breath. And no words need to be spoken.

It was such a marvelous discovery, just one breath at a time. It is the way life is. It is the way all manner of being is. Inspiration means breathing in. There is a rising and a falling, a clinging and a letting go in each breath. There is a dying and a resurrection in each breath. There is complete trust and dependency in each moment of life.

To pray with thinking and discerning (First Method), probing and comparing (Second Method) and then to pray by just being (Third Method) is the prayer of mystics and infants. To see without judging, to hear without evaluating - this is true contemplation.

This prayer of breathing can be rhythmic and measured or take a very different form being unmeasured and spontaneous. The awareness of one's breathing can lead to the awareness of one's heartbeat and then to the dramatic and equally quiet awareness of the world's rhythm.

ADDITIONAL DIRECTION. This is the same as in the first two methods.

PRAYER. This is the same as in the Second Method.

METHOD. To begin, one may say mentally one word "Our" while breathing one breath. Then on the word, "Father" take another breath. And continue to the end of that prayer. Initially, attention might be directed to the meaning of the word, or to the person addressed, similar to the Second Method. But by connecting a word of prayer to each breath and moving to the next word and next breath, the sacredness of breath and life is recognized as the essence of prayer. And the words become signs pointing to a greater reality. The Spirit of God breathes within you.

259. RULE I

Perform this breathing prayer along with the words of the Hail Mary.

260. RULE II

Anyone who wishes to spend more time in this form of prayer may use other worded prayers as The Soul of Christ, The Hail Holy Queen or the Creed.

THE MYSTERIES OF THE LIFE OF OUR LORD FOR THE SECOND WEEK

261. Some of the following scripture passages and their respective "Points" are included in the text of the Exercises and referred to by (Annotation #) which was Ignatius' style of numbering paragraphs. Other passages are optional selections with "Points" included for most meditations.

Once again be mindful that there need not be seven days in any one of Ignatius' labeled "Weeks". There are extra meditations and scripture references for each Week to be used as desired, since one retreatant may spend four days on the Second Week, another might pray for nine days. One might have four days in the Third Week, another might pray six.

262. THE ANNUNCIATION AND THE INCARNATION

LUKE 1: 26 - 38 # 101

FIRST POINT. The angel Gabriel visits Mary, "Rejoice, so highly favored, the Lord is with you. You are to conceive and bear a son, and you must name him Jesus."

SECOND POINT. The angel confirms what he had said by announcing, "And behold Elizabeth your kinswoman has in her old age, herself conceived a son."

THIRD POINT. Our Lady replied, "I am the handmaid of the Lord; let what you have said be done to me."

263. THE VISITATION OF OUR LADY

LUKE 1: 39 - 56

FIRST POINT. Mary visited Zechariah's house and greeted Elizabeth. Now as soon as Elizabeth heard Mary's greeting, the baby leapt in her womb. And Elizabeth was filled with the Holy Spirit, and she lifted up her voice with a loud cry and said, "Blessed art thou among women and blessed is the fruit of thy womb."

SECOND POINT. Mary responds, "My soul proclaims the greatness of the Lord."

THIRD POINT. Mary stayed with Elizabeth about three months.

264. THE BIRTH OF CHRIST OUR LORD
LUKE 2: 1 - 14 # 111

265. THE SHEPHERDS
LUKE 2: 8 - 20

FIRST POINT. The birth of Jesus was made known to the shepherds by an angel, "I bring to you news of great joy. Today in the town of David a savior has been born to you."

SECOND POINT. The shepherds go to Bethlehem. They went with haste and found Mary and Joseph and the baby lying in the manger.

THIRD POINT. The shepherds returned glorifying and praising God for all they had heard and seen. It was exactly as they had been told.

266. THE CIRCUMCISION
LUKE 2: 21

FIRST POINT. Jesus began his life following the prescription of the law for Jewish male infants.

SECOND POINT. He was named Jesus, as was foretold.

267. THE MAGI
MATTHEW 2: 1 - 12

FIRST POINT. Some wise men came to Jerusalem from the east. "We have seen his star as it rose and have come to do Him homage." "And you Bethlehem, in the land of Judah, out of you will come a leader who will shepherd my people."

SECOND POINT. They saw the child with his mother Mary and falling to their knees they worshiped him and offered him gifts of gold, frankincense and myrrh.

THIRD POINT. Being warned in a dream not to return to Herod, they withdrew to their own country by another way.

268. THE PRESENTATION
LUKE 2: 22 - 38 # 132

269. THE FLIGHT INTO EGYPT
MATTHEW 2: 13 - 18 # 132

270. THE RETURN FROM EGYPT

MATTHEW 2: 19 - 23

FIRST POINT. An angel appeared in a dream to Joseph, "Get up, take the child and his mother and go back to the land of Israel for those who wanted to kill the child are dead."

SECOND POINT. Taking the child and his mother, he went back to the land of Israel.

THIRD POINT. He learned that Archelaus, had succeeded his father Herod as ruler of Judea, and so they settled in a town called Nazareth. "He will be called a Nazarene."

271. THE LIFE OF JESUS AGE TWELVE TO THIRTY *# 134*

272. JESUS GOES UP TO THE TEMPLE AT THE AGE OF TWELVE *# 134*

273. THE BAPTISM OF CHRIST *# 158*
274. THE TEMPTATION OF CHRIST *# 161*

275. THE VOCATION OF THE APOSTLES *# 161*

276. THE FIRST MIRACLE AT THE MARRIAGE FEAST OF CANA IN GALILEE

JOHN 2: 1 - 11

FIRST POINT. Mary, Jesus and his disciples were invited to a wedding in Cana.

SECOND POINT. Mary confides to Jesus, "They have no wine." She then bids the servants, "Whatsoever He shall say to you, do."

THIRD POINT. Jesus said to the servants, "Fill the jars with water. Draw some out now and take it to the steward." The steward called the bridegroom and said, "You have kept the best wine until now."

277. CHRIST CASTS THE SELLERS FROM THE TEMPLE

JOHN 2: 13 - 22

FIRST POINT. Jesus did not approve of the law that forced people to pay for the blessing of Yahweh.

SECOND POINT. Jesus was disappointed in the common belief that conditions were placed on Yahweh's love for people.

THIRD POINT. Jesus showed his anger with the sellers who were taking advantage of the poor and flaunting their greed within the temple gates.

278. THE SERMON ON THE MOUNT # 161

279. CHRIST CALMS THE STORM

MATTHEW 8: 23 - 27

FIRST POINT. While Jesus was asleep in the boat a great storm arose.

SECOND POINT. His terrified disciples awaken Him, "Save us Lord, we are going down!"

THIRD POINT. With that He stood up and rebuked the winds and the sea and all was calm again. And they marveled saying, "What manner of man is this, that even the winds and the sea obey him?"

280. CHRIST WALKS UPON THE LAKE # 161

281. THE APOSTLES ARE SENT TO PREACH

MATTHEW 10: 1 - 16

FIRST POINT. Jesus summons His twelve disciples and gives them authority over unclean spirits with power to cure all kinds of diseases and sickness.

SECOND POINT. He tells them, "If anyone does not welcome you or listen to what you have to say, as you walk out of the house or town, shake the dust from your feet."

THIRD POINT. He gives them clear instructions, tells them which communities to direct their attention and teaches them prudence and patience, "Remember I am sending you forth as sheep into the midst of wolves. Be as cunning as serpents and as harmless as doves."

282. THE CONVERSION OF MAGDALENE

LUKE 7: 36 - 50

FIRST POINT. Magdalene, carrying an alabaster jar of ointment, waited behind Jesus at his feet. He was dining in the house of a Pharisee.

SECOND POINT. Magdalene's tears fell on His feet, and she wiped them away with her hair. She covered His feet with kisses and anointed them with ointment.

THIRD POINT. Jesus said to the pharisee, "Her many sins must have been forgiven her or she would not have shown such great love." And to Mary He said, "Your faith has saved you, go in peace."

283. CHRIST FEEDS FIVE THOUSAND
MATTHEW 14: 13 - 21
FIRST POINT. Since it was getting late, the disciples asked Jesus to dismiss the multitude of people who were with Him. Jesus replied, "There is no need for them to go, give them something to eat yourselves."

SECOND POINT. Jesus said, "Bring the five loaves and two fish to me." He raised his eyes to heaven and said the blessing. And breaking the bread he gave it to his disciples who gave it to the crowds.

THIRD POINT. They all ate and had their fill, and they collected the fragments that were left over, twelve full baskets.

284. THE TRANSFIGURATION
MATTHEW 17: 1 - 9
FIRST POINT. Jesus took Peter, James and and his brother John and led them up a high mountain. His face became resplendent as the sun and His garments like snow.

SECOND POINT. He spoke with Moses and Elijah. Peter said he would like to build three tents, one for you, one for Moses and one for Elijah.

THIRD POINT. A voice was heard from heaven, saying, "This is my beloved Son, Hear ye him." When the disciples heard this voice, they fell down for fear, their faces to the ground. Jesus came and touched them, and said to them, "Stand up and do not be afraid."

285. THE RAISING OF LAZARUS # 161

286. THE SUPPER AT BETHANY

MATTHEW 26: 6 - 10

FIRST POINT. Our Lord eats with Lazarus in the house of Simon the leper.

SECOND POINT. Mary pours out the ointment on the head of Christ.

THIRD POINT. The disciples were indignant, "Why this waste?" But Jesus defends Mary saying, "Why are you upsetting this woman? She has performed a great kindness to me. In fact her good deed will be proclaimed wherever the good news is preached."

287. PALM SUNDAY *# 161*

288. JESUS PREACHES IN THE TEMPLE *# 161*

THE MYSTERIES OF THE LIFE OF OUR LORD FOR THE THIRD WEEK

289. THE LAST SUPPER # *190*

290. FROM THE LAST SUPPER TO THE AGONY IN THE GARDEN # *200*

291. FROM THE GARDEN TO THE HOUSE OF ANNAS # *208*

292. FROM THE HOUSE OF ANNAS TO THE HOUSE OF CAIPHAS # *208*

293. FROM THE HOUSE OF CAIPHAS TO THE HOUSE OF PILATE # *208*

294. FROM THE HOUSE OF PILATE TO THE HOUSE OF HEROD # *208*

295. FROM THE HOUSE OF HEROD TO THAT OF PILATE # *208*

296. FROM THE HOUSE OF PILATE TO THE CROSS # *208*

297. JESUS DIES ON THE CROSS # *208*

298. FROM THE CROSS TO THE SEPULCHRE # *208*

THE PASSION AS A WHOLE
MATT. 26 - 27; MARK 14 - 15; LUKE 22 - 23; JOHN 18 - 19

THE MYSTERIES OF THE LIFE OF OUR LORD FOR THE FOURTH WEEK

299. THE FIRST APPARITION TO OUR LADY # 218

300. THE SECOND APPARITION TO MARY MAGDALENE MARK 16: 1 - 11

301. THE THIRD APPARITION TO THE TWO MARYS
MATTHEW 28: 1 - 10

302. THE FOURTH APPARITION TO PETER
LUKE 24: 9 - 12, 33 - 34

303. THE FIFTH APPARITION ON THE ROAD TO EMMAUS
LUKE 24: 13 - 35

304. THE SIXTH APPARITION TO THE DISCIPLES
JOHN 20: 19 - 25

305. THE SEVENTH APPARITION TO THOMAS
JOHN 20: 24 - 29

306. THE EIGHTH APPARITION TO SEVEN DISCIPLES
JOHN 21: 1 - 17

307. THE NINTH APPARITION ON MT TABOR
MATTHEW 28: 16 - 20

308. THE TENTH APPARITION TO THE FIVE HUNDRED
I CORINTHIANS 15: 6

309. THE ELEVENTH APPARITION TO JAMES

I CORINTHIANS 15: 7

310. THE TWELFTH APPARITION
TO JOSEPH OF ARIMATHEA

311. THE THIRTEENTH APPARITION TO PAUL
I CORINTHIANS 15:8

312. THE ASCENSION OF CHRIST OUR LORD
ACTS 1: 1 - 12

PENTECOST
ACTS 2: 1 - 11, JOHN 20: 19 - 23

313. RULES FOR THE DISCERNMENT OF SPIRITS

When one decides to make a long retreat and suddenly surrenders a large block of time away from his community, family and friends and is also denied his usual interests and labors, various reactions occur within the retreatant. With many hours of private time dedicated to quiet reflection and soul searching exercises there is bound to be some strain as the mind and body adjust to such a rigorous schedule. To be sensitive to the different feelings and movements within the heart and soul while one is busy about the work of the Exercises is an essential component of the retreatant's daily Examens and the heart of the sharing with the Director. The interior stirrings and impressions of the First Week will definitely differ from those of the succeeding week, so special attention must be given to these movements of the spirit. "What's going on?" is an inside and outside question. It is at once practical, emotional and spiritual. It is the gist of discernment of your spirit.

314. APPROPRIATE INSPIRATIONS

With a great number of individuals who make the Exercises, the Spirit works with compassionate invitations and straight guidelines to the path of wholeness and freedom. The consolation is characterized with great clarity of reason, strong desires and firm resolutions.

For those who have been unduly influenced and pressured by persons in their family, religion or society their hunger for spiritual freedom becomes starkly evident. The desire to detach from such obsessions and become the person God created and called each one to be becomes evident.

For those overwhelmed in the competition for worldly approval, progress and pride, the Spirit reveals another way of life that is peaceful and attainable.

For those who have been living a life that was really not of their own choosing, a life on someone else's terms, or an unreflective life, the Spirit offers a new chance, a pearl of great price, a graced life and promises to be faithful. While there are many good inspirations there are typical doubts for this First Week. Is this way of life too good to be true? How will I know? Will I be able to persevere? Will I have to give up my stimulations, attachments and addictions permanently? Is it enough for me to just be my true self? How can I be sure?

315. PERSONAL MOTIVATIONS

Many retreatants begin the journey of the Spiritual Exercises with the desire to become more perfect, more prayerful, more aware and to be outstanding in their service of God our Lord. The rules for discernment are quite different from those of the previous Annotation.

For these retreatants, consolation is characterized emotionally, by feelings of tranquillity and patience, intellectually, with understanding and acceptance of one's weaknesses and limitations.

Moments of desolation or anxiety may be discovered from the subtle intention to try harder or to be better than God made me, not noticing the competitive or comparative tendency to outperform or to pray and act somewhat perfectly. The desire to get as much as possible out of life or out of each day can reveal one's intensity to make things happen. And so being driven to live up to my own expectations or standards will lead to some disappointment or sadness.

316. CONSOLATION

Consolation may be called a God feeling or a heavenly feeling, but it is truly an earthly feeling.

Consolation is a quiet and clear awareness of harmony in one's life, a feeling of well being. It may be compared to a healthy child's unassuming sense of being precious and loveable. When consolation is present, it is not an overwhelming feeling, but rather a subsisting presence, as simple as air, sunlight or sky. In the midst of the variety of daily activities and problems that surface each day, consolation can persist without disturbance.

The peace within the person is spontaneous and unrelated to a particular person, event or circumstance. The joy within the person is not connected to success or achievement. It has no previous cause, but seems rather to pervade the person. It is a spirit that encourages and nourishes; it renews itself as it radiates. Consolation does not depend on a particular idea, person or thing, yet there is a certain message communicated that life has its own mysterious meaning.

Consolation can be a sensory experience but it always involves an interior appreciation of one's experience.

While identification with the unfortunate and tragic side of life can bring about strong feelings of anger, disgust and despair, even at times like that there can be a profound sense of unity with the poor, the violated, the imprisoned, the homeless, the refugees. One sees them as God does, as Jesus did, that God truly accompanies them in their misery. With this awareness our response to suffering humanity can be compassionate and constructive. Without this graced view, depression and revenge seem justifiable.

Finally, consolation lifts me above and beyond the details and the mundane. It is an "in the world but not of the world" kind of experience. It makes everything seem to fit. It is like seeing the tapestry of one's life. The joys and sorrows, the ups and downs bring texture and quality to life. There is an invitation to see not only visually but with heart-optics, with the spirit of truth.

With the realization that one is human, weak and fragile, there is not a negative reaction, but a certainty of being holy, just as I am, right where I am - experiencing the ordinary things of life without ambition or greed.

There are daily increases in faith, hope and love. In spiritual consolation the person feels attracted to what is wholesome and energized to act on behalf of peace.

317. DESOLATION

Ignatius defines desolation simply as "the opposite of consolation". Where there is positive and light in consolation, there is negativity and darkness in desolation. While there is clarity of perception in the experience of consolation, there is confusion and uncertainty in one's perceptions during desolation.

And so if we are trying to decide and then act in this state of desolation our divisive thoughts will prevail. Decisions could tend to be short-sighted, reactionary or pessimistic. Retreat is an especially opportune time to understand desolation - including the signs, pressures and results that typify our periods of desolation. Because people on retreat are usually quieter, more reflective and more introspective than at other times, this is a great opportunity.

The most insignificant actions performed during times of consolation seem to produce extraordinary fruit and satisfaction, whereas with desolation, nothing seems really valuable. One goes through the motions and wonders if there is any merit, logic or purpose in proceeding. In desolation one senses the burdens of life; even the elements seem out of harmony - the earth seems stagnant and the air unstable. In periods of consolation the same earth presents a firm foundation and the air seems fresh and buoyant.

During desolation there can be a noticeable sense of judgment as one tends to blame anyone or anything for his lack of well being. We might accuse ourselves of procrastination, laziness or lethargy as we assume incorrectly the causes of our depressed feelings. There can be a tendency to blame others but what we may not realize is that the spirit is simply unwell; as the body goes through low points so does the spirit.

At times like this it seems impossible that one could actually appreciate the experience or allow it to be beneficial. Yet, the sense of loss, weakness and helplessness, the feeling of inadequacy and unworthiness, can be very effective. What an opportunity to identify with the poor and the disenfranchised without the actual dire straits! Desolation gives us the chance to be aware that we are wounded healers. It is possible to use this experience for effective growth.

The approach to desolation and the experience of desolation itself are critical elements during the retreat. It is important to share not only these feelings with the director but also to discuss one's facility or difficulty in integrating them with daily life. The desolation experience, like physical pain or personal rejection, can be a valuable preparation for life and growth. As part of the microcosm of life, it is neither to be glorified nor condemned, but understood and dealt with carefully.

To be able to recognize the signs of desolation in one's own life and in the life of another is a great gift, just as if one were to recognize rain clouds and be able to dress accordingly. To remember not to make any changes or major decisions is essential until this phase is passed, just as it is wise to refrain from expressing your anger when you are out of control. It is so important to be led by the truth, to see the good in all things before one makes a decision, and to act with an attitude of consolation. The attitude is the message! God calls us to be joyful people, so our Godlike decisions arc those that bring joy to ourselves and to those around us.

Rules For Discernment

In order to work through this negative state it is necessary to discover the cause of the feelings. The first type of desolation comes from the deprivation of basic physical and emotional needs. If we are hungry, tired or lacking proper shelter for prolonged periods of time we can enter into a state of desolation. However, even after being fed we can still feel the effects of hunger so the feelings associated with these needs take a while to subside as well. If two or more of these needs are present simultaneously the effects are amplified.

Just as our bodies can wear down, our emotions can tire from stressful encounters. We need some freshness and vitality to regain control of our lives. At times we feel lonely or there is a lack of intimacy in our lives. We are unable to relate our daily story or we feel as though no one understands or cares. As little children we were listened to, held and loved. But as adults we have had to become independent and must pay the price for this freedom. Maybe we were taught that we no longer needed intimacy. But we are still loving people and there is a child in each of us. We are still God's children, thoroughly human and God wants us to have affective lives. God wants us to give generously of ourselves and receive openly from others. Without this we become cold, unGodlike and uncompassionate. We need to be in touch with reality, with real people. Fantasy, wishful thinking and pious thoughts are not appropriate substitutes. They may replace other essential needs but they cannot take the place of intimacy. It is interesting to note that we are capable of regulating our time and activities but our spirit is meant to soar.

And our hearts can only be happy with a true and intimate response to life.

A second type of desolation is caused by powerful, unconscious experiences. An addictive personality might have unusual assaults on his spirit that require strong and available resources. First, just as a healthy diabetic can distinguish whether he needs some sugar, rest, medicine or help, so too the particular side effects of addiction require a sensitivity to one's bodily and emotional needs. Second, there is a need for persons in the community who are understanding, knowledgeable and enthusiastic about their response to this individual. Third, a healthy prayer life can bring nourishment and provide an immediate interior assurance that the person is not alone.

Just as an addiction is a sense of physical or chemical deprivation, greed presents mental signals that tell the person "I don't
have enough; I need more; I need it to be happy; if I only had this
thing I would be satisfied." Greed instigates intense pressure and
fallacious hopes that never satisfy. Grasping unexpectedly, on a
daily basis for unusual things, is not atypical. Because of the
ensuing guilt, the person often detaches himself compulsively
and treats the object attained as the source of the craving.

The most helpful therapy not only convinces the person that he
is not deprived but helps him discover what he actually has.
Greed is thus based on a misconception, sometimes dramatic,
sometimes subtle. The cure is to see clearly. It is sometimes radical, but it is always effective.

A third frequent cause of desolation is judgment. When someone judges himself, he has split his being into a judiciary that
evaluates and a victim on trial. If someone judges another, he
mentally splits the Body of Christ and designates himself as the
tribunal of justice and metes out a sentence on the other. One
alternates between praise and exoneration to rejection and punishment. We have learned how to divide ourselves and others.
This is the prerequisite for judging. This always causes desolation in the judge and can be instrumental in bringing about desolation in the person judged.

People who have such consciences are constantly legislating
ideals by which to measure themselves. They have an interior
parole board that judges whether or not they have lived up to par.
They frequently fluctuate between the false grandeur of pride
and the devastating experience of guilt.

318. DISCERNMENT

One of the essentials of discernment is described by Ignatius,
"In time of desolation never make any change in the decision to
which we adhered in the preceding consolation." This is consistent with the notion of being led only by three notions: consolation, the clarity of truth, and finding God in all things. And while
we have dark and doubtful days in work, relationships and
prayer, these are not times for decisions or resolutions.

During periods of desolation we will receive suggestions that
seem to promise a quick release from the malaise and confusion,
but frequently they are destructive. They are definitely not a

reflection of our best self.

Somehow when we are experiencing desolation it is as though something very basic is lacking. Yet we cannot locate the area of deprivation. It would be so easy if we realized that we were hungry and it was affecting our mind, or exhausted and it was skewing our emotional reactions to normal stimuli.

In desolation the heaviness or imbalance is not as easy to locate so we need some special procedures for healthy functioning. People with chronic illnesses can identify with the descriptions and the prescriptions Ignatius provides for those in desolation.

When things seem more and more complex, keep it simple; that is the way God made it. While matter is compounded and quantified, our spirit is simple. It helps to remember that on occasions like this.

319. ACTIONS DURING DESOLATION

There are three things that Ignatius refers to regarding appropriate actions during times of desolation. While patience is essential to work out the answer to many problems and questions in life, three actions are indicated for these times of desolation: meditation, self-examination and creative stimulation.

First, meditation calms our anxieties and enables us to face our particular problem with less emotion, less distraction and less desperation for a solution. To view our life from a distant, deep and different perspective can provide a quiet and detached approach. Not seeing clearly and acting chaotically is a normal reaction when one is in a state of panic; so if one can be patient many problems can be prevented.

Second, when hopes and dreams do not unfold as planned, some people could become psychologically disturbed and dysfunctional. So Ignatius mentions the importance of diagnosing whether this is stress due to the lack of basic needs being satisfied, or confused thoughts, or is it actually spiritual desolation.

When things are going along smoothly there is no need to change; when they are not, it is time to intensify one's activity, examine one's behavior and take note of the interior reactions to stimuli. It is a special time to step back and get a different perspective.

Third, Ignatius recommends stimulation - wake-up sort of activities that refreshen a person. Regular physical work and mental exercise provide some variety for the mind and body. What is it that you could do for yourself emotionally that would be most invigorating? As you come up with a few suggestions the most obvious ones will surface as you provide your own best remedy. Compute your blessings, create a personal schedule, contact an old friend, take an unusual nature walk, visit a special person, read a good book, register for an interesting course, etc.

And so with an atmosphere of patience the three types of activity during a time of desolation, meditation, self-examination and suitable creative stimulation (penance) can each be practiced with beneficial results.

320. SPECIAL HELPS DURING DESOLATION

Desolation may be compared to the feeling of rejection, loss, or incompetence. These are not considered to be desirable feelings, yet desolation can be a unique opportunity to grow in wisdom and grace. The challenge during desolation requires special endurance and training, otherwise it can be overwhelming.

First, it is important to be aware of your own natural gifts and powers. On many occasions, you handle problems with family, friends, co-workers and superiors successfully. When you are unsuccessful you experience a period of trial and error. This can lead to growth and to a level of maturity as you discover your strengths and limitations. Sometimes there is a positive and spontaneous reaction to an adversity. At other times the process is slow and complicated as you learn to cope effectively.

Ignatius suggests that the retreatant recall how much resilience he has, as well as the occasions in the past when his approaches resulted in consolation and good effects. To see, even in spiritual desolation, that there are convenient and concrete human reactions that can bring about a change helps the retreatant to realize that he already has the required resources at his disposal. This awareness instills confidence.

An honest appraisal of the conditions affecting the person during desolation helps to select the prognosis as well as the remedy. When a person feels no "abundance of fervor" and does not have any sense of overflowing love or favor from God we have the symptoms of desolation. Yet, how often have people not felt favored? Did you realize you were experiencing desolation? To readily admit that some of these feelings have persisted for a long time and that this actual experience is complex, unanswerable and deeply disappointing is helpful reality testing. When there is such darkness there is no light. Self direction is impossible and any movement, even inactivity seems dangerous. Light without limitation or definition creates a white-out effect.

Thus, accepting the reality of the situation is at least a beginning, with truth as a first step. Desolation is a reality that one does not cause, is no one's fault and can not be prevented. We simply live in darkness and light, and sometimes there will be an over concentration of one or the other that envelops us.

To understand or believe that you are infinitely loved, carefully created and specifically sent by God into the world at this very moment is profoundly consoling. You are not alone because even as you seemingly face yourself alone, you are filled with God's love, God's favor, God's grace and God's presence.

321. PATIENCE BASED ON TRUST

This consideration can bring the retreatant to the conclusion "that consolation will soon return" just as the sun is sure to rise. This increases confidence as the retreatant goes about his work despite the desolation that is still present. Patience and action seem to be the answers to so many problems and questions in life: our own life and in the life of society.

It is common advice to say, "Take it easy, don't strain, things will get better and be patient." But it is a remarkable grace when one can live it under stressful conditions. Have you noticed how pleasantly surprised you are when you are able to stay calm during situations that used to disturb you? It is as though an event that previously controlled you, no longer has power over you. What a nice surprise! Where did the anxiety go? How did I overcome it? How did it lose its power over me? Is it really true that when I have a true perspective, problems that seemed overwhelming are less significant and less threatening?

The first step is to see the craving for a quick solution as self defeating.

322. CAUSES OF DESOLATION

Why do people experience desolation? In his Spiritual Exercises Ignatius gives three principal reasons.

The first reason is a neglect of physical or mental exercise; a lack of intimacy or time for quiet reflection could also be a cause. People often become distracted by life as though they were help-lessly riding on a roller coaster or being taken for a ride expect-ing something to happen. It is as though the earth is moving and they are being passively carried along, but there is no self activ-ity. This may be typified by a stagnancy, a clinging to a routine without any discernible reflection. This experience of periodic distress might be described as a numbness to life, an inactivity of the heart and mind. The word "depression" was not in Ignatius' vocabulary, but he might have applied it with some reservations had it been in vogue. This state can sometimes be camouflaged from oneself and from others. The person might appear to be secure while he is actually clinging; and he might seem to be actively involved while he is near panic.

Therapeutic exercises are required, ones that involve a con-scious exchange where the person is fully aware of giving and receiving. It is important to develop a sensitivity to life so that he is feeling joy and sorrow with body and heart. In this way he can respond to the joys and the humor with light heartedness, and to the pain and injustice with words that are supportive and actions that are appropriate. This kind of involvement with life, feelings and people can bring an immediate lift from desolation to con-solation. To be fully engaged with life assumes the ability to relax and take time each day to nourish oneself. The body is restored through sleep and then it becomes hungry for life and its challenges. The ability to relax while one is awake is a special gift that nourishes the spirit and rests the nerves. As the body requires motion, these centers need recharging: the heart needs stimulation, the spirit needs life and the mind needs ideas.

The second reason a person goes through desolation is testing. It would be unusual if every time we took a test we scored 100. No one recalls every detail in a book or attends a large social gathering and remembers everyone's name. Awareness of every-thing is impossible and not human. We become aware of our limitations because they are there. If you ever took a test with-out studying, you found out just how much you recalled from merely listening in class. Once you have missed a plane connec-tion you soon realize how fallible the world, and everyone in it, is. The fact that we do not recall names on first hearing, without sufficient time, association, or repetition to assist us, is quite normal. We keep discovering our abilities and limitations. Gradually, we make ongoing adjustments through acceptance, evaluation and reality testing.

What an interesting and natural experience: trial and error! We are tested by life and sometimes we administer the test ourselves. Our feelings, attitudes and our spirituality are questioned. What a wonderful chance for investigation and discovery!

A third reason we experience desolation is that it helps us come to a truer knowledge of ourselves. We realize that we are not the cause of our being. We did not create ourselves. There is a real powerlessness inherent to us. We observe that we are not in charge of our life or of even one day - not even a single breath. This truth leads us to something special, to discover that everything that I am and have is gift. It was given to me, it is given to me and it will be given to me.

Life is a relative gift. It has a type, size, measure and quality. It can be looked at in subjective ways, but it comes from love and it comes from God. This gift includes everything that was and everything that is, beginning with the least detail, and up to and including the greatest asset. Therefore there are no reasons for being unduly proud. I am connected to something bigger than myself. My life is not my own, even though I am a center. It is very consoling because I do not need to measure my goodness or my accomplishments. And while I can marvel for what has been and for what is, I do not have to prove anything to myself, to the world, and certainly not to God.

As my strengths are gifts, so are my weaknesses, limitations, faults and inclinations. That is very consoling. It is a freeing, redeeming, forgiving, amnesty-like reality of which only God, only one like Jesus could convince us. It is our privilege to believe in this immense love. To preach this gift of unconditional love to the ends of the earth is our shared vocation.

323. THOUGHTS DURING CONSOLATION

When one is enjoying consolation it is a good time to do some organizing for the future, rather than simply riding high and feeling invulnerable. During this joyful time one can store up some energy, use foresight and reflect on the problem of desolation. Sometimes it is easy to work and to communicate, to give and to receive. While in the state of consolation, everything seems gratifying and possible, even successful. But no one is always in this state, so it is a good time to accept this fact. Climbing a mountain is not always fun and coming down is not always exhilarating.

So, recall your own reactions when you have faced adversity, resistance and obstacles. During consolation, clarify your plan, and store up some emotional reserves. By accepting the reality of the past, you are taking into account eventualities and possibilities; you are very realistic. Realizing that there is much more to happiness then temporary gratification, is a mature approach to life. Sometimes habits of the past, superficial feelings or pressures from obligations rule our behavior. Rather than give in to this mode of behavior and face the subsequent desolation, if we have previously prepared for such occurrences we will see a more complete picture. My better self will help me to do what I really desire and what is for my best interest. Our minds and hearts help us to enjoy the fruits of our time and energy.

324. BEING REALISTIC

There are some Scripture passages where Jesus relates a story about preparing for future events and for difficult times. When you construct a house He advises the builder to examine the terrain to be sure it is on a sturdy and firm foundation. Jesus recalls how an army going into battle is sure to examine its resources in comparison to those of one's enemy. Is there a good chance of winning? Will you honestly be better off after this experience than at the present time?

Utilize your intelligence and reason, and trust in God during periods of desolation. It is important to remember that you have the same grace of God regardless of your attitude or emotional state, but in times of consolation the grace is more tangible.

325. CHARACTERISTICS
OF DESOLATION

During desolation the person must perceive when it is happening, be able to describe what is occurring and be confident enough to express these periods to one's director. For while they can be disturbing experiences, they present opportunities for growth and self understanding. In consolation, we feel acceptance by the world and from God; in desolation we feel like the world is not cooperating, there is resistance and static. We do not seem to see, hear or feel clearly; God seems distant. We do not even feel in tune with our family, friends or even with our own bodies; there are obstacles everywhere we turn.

So it is normal to go through phases like this and to feel that I am working against myself, that I am not thoroughly together. There seems to be strain and lack of control; in fact I wonder if I am crazy as my heart wants me to act but it does not seem to be present in my activity. I want to withdraw, back off, or be more passive. At other times I prefer to be more dependent on others since I am mistrustful and insecure with my own choices.

When I am independent and centered, when I feel free and aware, I can be securely interdependent and ask others for advice. Certainly two people can do things that one person cannot, and a group of people can do things that two cannot. So when I am aware and confident of my own strength, I can recognize the potential and accomplishment of others without feeling fearful, inferior, dependent or needing approval. So while my choice is to preserve my independence and my freedom, I can accept help from others. But when I am fearful, I observe the world through the filters of anxiety and I do not see reality. We accomplish so little when we are anxious or fearful; sometimes we cannot act, speak, think clearly or feel other emotions.

In times of desolation we notice that fear and discouragement can rule our lives. Since there is sufficient storage of courage and strength to withstand this period of crisis, it is good to realize that these reactions are normal and that this phase shall pass. Finally the simple statement, "be not afraid" is appropriate and reminds us that we are fragile human creatures and our thinking, feeling and acting can easily be contaminated by fear.

Desolation is like riding through a storm at sea. We might lower the sails, close the hatches and patiently hang on, ready to act when the coast is clear and the sea is calm. It does not help to curse the storm except in expressing one's frustrations; it does not help to condemn the course we have chosen, but hopefully we will discover something from this trial.

When you respond out of fear and give license to this unruly emotion, it is like giving a fearful person power - frightening things happen. When people are forced into submission by others, or manipulated by circumstances, they often will repeat this behavior when the positions are reversed. The damage is similar. When people have been deprived, abused and forced to submit, it is obvious that violence will take a further toll. When the opportunity arises for a release of this enslavement, frequently the tyrranical pattern is repeated involuntarily. Conditioned responses can become the normal way of life. The victims are seemingly powerless and defenseless.

326. TRUE AND FALSE LOVE

Ignatius compares the behavior of one who is in love with a person who is greedy. Someone who loves is joyful, sharing and wants to express his feelings to the one he loves, to friends and to the world. There is a desire to be open, to announce this good news. His candor, care and compassion are transparent. No amount of energy expended is too much, no degree of apparent sacrifice is too great. When a person loves, he wants to give all his possessions and some that are not his: life, the future, the moon, one's heart. There is no desire to hide this complete offering, nor to seek some reward or thanks because this very offering delights the heart of the lover.

On the other hand there are different traits for false lovers: seductiveness, insecurity, secretiveness and greediness. He sees something he wants and he will do anything to get it. At times some surface actions and words are similar to those of the true lover. Each appears to be willing to sacrifice anything or everything for the other. Yet one is based on pride and violence and the other is founded on spirit and peace. Although the forms of behavior and the words are comparable, the intention and state of the person must be examined. Truly, by their fruit shall you know them! See if you can notice the anxiety, confusion or ambivalence in the behavior. In one there is ignorance and manipulation, yet the desire and attraction are authentic if not desperate. As with someone who is starved, so with someone who is bereft of love; each needs to escape this deprivation. Caring for the other is not the intention; the goal is to possess, to take care of one's personal needs at the expense of another.

There are many ways of testing for real love. Love is real if one is ready to forgive. Love is observed and tested in the way one overcomes the obstacles that come between the lover and beloved. Love is real if it is simple, like finding God in all things.

Hence, the one who loves does not envision distance or time, parents, work or wealth as hindrances, but sees each factor as an occasion for expressing his love to the beloved.

327. RESTLESSNESS OR TRANQUILLITY

Can you tell the difference between a false and true lover? For the false lover there is a wall to be stormed, a prize to be won, a battle to be fought; it is as though a person is speaking of a war, with a battlefield, weapons and terms for the conquest and final victory. For the true lover there is no conflict, achievement, defeat or victory - only peace. There is no winner or loser - only oneness, for they are not two. So the true lover sees things as one, and reality as so many parts of the whole.

The degree of lightness and darkness in one's life might be compared to the peace of a loving relationship versus the anxiety of an unsatisfying relationship. Constant joy and surprise pervades when one truly loves, whereas with false loves there are doubts and suspicions at every turn.

In our relationship with God there is a mixture of light and darkness, confidence and doubt, surprise and boredom, peace and anxiety. Do you ever doubt your unique lovableness and goodness? Do you question the loving presence and unconditional acceptance of God? Are you anxious about your relationship or closeness to God? How often do you tend to measure and how often are you absolutely assured?

Desolation can occur in an instant when we try to measure the immeasurable, when we seek or demand signs from ourselves, others, life or God. We are not greater than, nor above, creation. We cannot manipulate life and expect to satisfy all our needs. We cannot call forth magic signs and convince ourselves that they are from the creator of the universe, when we know they are our own projections and delusions. While it is more difficult to tease ourselves mentally than it is to tickle ourselves physically, it is a common practice.

328. RULES FOR DISCERNMENT OF SPIRITS

SECOND WEEK

As the retreatant progresses to the Second Week of retreat there appear different interior movements than occurred in the First Week. The following should help in a more accurate discernment of these spirits.

329. CLARITY OF PERCEPTION

It is characteristic of God's grace acting on the soul to give true happiness and spiritual joy and to banish all sadness and disturbance. Desolation occurs when the retreatant thinks and feels that while there might be happiness and consolation, it is short-lived or not sufficiently satisfying. This deceptive reasoning is subtle, because there is truth in the fact that everything is temporary and no one thing can satisfy the heart. When the retreatant can see through this type of distraction he will have very few things to fear.

330. REAL OR APPARENT GOOD

Ignatius mentions that God alone can give consolation to the soul, without any previous cause. There are other types of consolation that come from certain things we do or from events that happen to us. People are not in command of consolation though they follow a routine of good behavior and good habits. They may receive praise from others for good behavior and rewards for noteworthy achievement and they still may not feel consoled. So it is an interesting statement that real consolation is given to the heart and soul by God. This joy of the Creator's presence feels as though all actions are flowing directly from the love of God. We can move from a state of discouragement to consolation, then wonder how it happens. After hours of work we can also feel simply tired and not consoled. It is an interesting observation that true consolation is pure gift from God and not caused by ourselves or others.

To those who are awake and sensitive, the consolation that lasts, that is effective, that does the work of the spirit, that brings peace and joy to people is very clear. But if people do not evaluate and trust their own senses, they can be fooled by the apparent good, or fallacious arguments that surround them. This is also true in less dramatic situations when I repeat a habit that was traditionally good or apparently good. If I do not reflect on my intentions I might fool myself into thinking I am doing good.

In war, direct commands from authority dictate that blowing up a village will bring peace. If the person could imagine the suffering of people and the loss to their community, he would have to question the reasonableness of this order. Was it deception, pride, fear or power? How does God feel about such destruction? Is the person really convinced in his own mind and heart that this is truly bringing peace?

If a person does not reflect on war and see its effects, he might be deluded into thinking that killing and murder are a greater good. He may reason it is beneficial because he is helping the government, is being paid, is supporting his family, or is getting medals for it. "Service Medals," they are ironically called. Can you imagine? Service! Those who invaded Lebanon, Afghanistan, Grenada, and Kosovo received service medals. Were they serving God, peace, love and non-violence, or were they serving the private interest groups of their particular governments?

Sometimes we do that with ourselves; we give ourselves little righteous or prayer medals. It is important to find out if this is the good spirit or is this the spirit of the world that once again has frozen our thinking.

One of the ways of checking the truth and goodness of my actions is in being aware of my anticipation. Am I looking forward to doing this, or can I feel my hesitation and reservations? Do I have doubts that this is what I really want or whether this is honestly a good thing for me to do? Afterwards, am I relieved that this obligation or event is over? This is the first sign that not only am I not doing God's will but it is not bringing lasting joy. Questions to ask myself that will reveal my integrity and honesty include the following. Do I have any regrets? Do I try to forget my participation? Can I enjoy what occurred, share it and celebrate it? In little things like visiting one's grandchild or niece, is there anticipation before going, am I excited while being with the child and is there a wonderful flavor that lasts long after the visit?

Consolation is quite easy to discern for people who are aware. But for those who are caught up in habits of obedience, righteousness, fear and approval, it will take some practice. These spiritual exercises are meant to help.

331. FEELINGS, REWARDS AND IDEALS

Ignatius talks about the difference between lightness and darkness. How do you detect the difference between a suggestion that brings consolation and one that distracts from goodness and truth? The latter is a temptation because of the destructive nature or perverse reactions that can be seen or felt by looking at the results in the whole context of the experience. And so there are three ways that people are tempted to do things that are neither in their own best interest, nor for the common good.

First, there is an natural desire for a good feeling or even a thrill and one of the easiest ways of being satisfied is through the approval of others. It is faster than achievement and more rapid than basic pleasures as eating or drinking. It is often visible, audible, tangible and intellectual. Some people experience these spontaneous highs because someone praised the work they had done. There was a brief gratifying feeling that quickly disappears. So while it is important to examine our feelings after receiving praise be sure to notice how long the feeling lasted.

Second, we are easily persuaded by rewards. When someone offers a prize, witness how many enter the contest hoping that they will win. But even though some may want the reward they may neglect to calculate the cost. When the focus is on a future prize, we are distracted from life in the present and do not see the surrender of time and self involved. And so a bribe is a gift given to you that exacts an incredible price that can jeopardize what you believe in and what you live for. The best way to evaluate a bribe is to reflect on one's experience to see what is truly exchanged in the process.

Otherwise as in the war analogy, the tendency might be simply to idealize the glories of war and miss the reality of the lives lost and the indescribable suffering endured.

Third, when we are tempted to perform according to some fascinating ideal, the dream provides a delightful escape, yet reality contains a basic joy and intrigue that is more tangible and more satisfying. The desire to surpass ourselves, to become better than we are is a dangerous ploy and begins with the rejection of our present self. To become more of anything is the subtlest of temptations for it is a direct appeal to the ego. It entails the total rejection of who I am and who I have been. Ideals can be so totally absorbing that I can miss the self that is being enslaved. While trying to achieve ideals, whether lofty or humble, the consequence can be frustration or pride. We go from a mighty goal to discouragement.

Here is another illusion. People frequently reset their ideals and as they strive they subjugate themselves and patterns of depression are noticed. Desolation is present. And the person can not see through these illusions because the ideals seem so laudable. The craving to become someone better is an endless treadmill of inadequacy, rejection and unceasing effort. The result is an unusual combination of shyness (fear) and pride (righteousness).

332. WARNING SIGNS

The enemies of light and peace are clear to objective observers and to those who are awake, but it is almost impossible for the indoctrinated to be awakened from their illusions.

Four recognizable sources of evil actions are obligation, condemnation, secrecy and fanaticism.

Condemning is one of the initial signs. It is unGodlike, unChristlike and unloving. It is a sign of rage and when combined with power can cause havoc and human destruction. Second, when people act under obligation or oblige others, they are not acting according to their hearts. They are insecure and are responding to some other power that threatens them. Some "must" or "have to" is coercing the person. They sometimes use positive words like duty and responsibility, but it is still slavery, and unbecoming of a loved human being. The third sign is secrecy carried to the point of deception. Devious purposes and covert actions can only be carried out in a clandestine manner, so secrecy and darkness are typical modes for people of destruction. The fourth sign is akin to patriotism, a passionate obsession to a concept, fanaticism. People who become overwhelmed by an ideal can envision the validity of their goals and destroy anyone or anything in the name of this ideal. They speak and act as though they are drugged while they consider themselves visionaries. They are far more concerned about their ideas about life than life itself.

333. TRACKING THE TRUTH

When one is dissatisfied with one's life, Ignatius suggests a thorough self examination of the course of one's thoughts and actions. If you can discover your feelings and thoughts at the outset, what sustained them in the process and what they consisted of at the end you may easily discover the cause of your unsatisfactory attitude.

Regarding your behavior, if you find that at the beginning you were tentative about a particular act's value, identify your doubt and clarify what it is. If you can recall that in the midst or at the conclusion of your activity you observed something that disturbed your peace or took tranquillity away or was contrary to what you truly want in life, take note and make the necessary adjustments.

334. TEMPTATIONS

Once you are able to trace what causes the disturbance, there is a certain amount of joy as you see how your thinking and actions have been influenced. Ignatius says that it is helpful to review the whole course of the temptation. At the moment of the particular attraction there was a seduction from the path you truly desire. It was under the guise of good, it was appealing, but it was not you. You were unduly influenced because you had not reflected sufficiently about what you really desire.

Examine how your good thoughts and normal tendency were weakened by this attractive bribe, reward or ideal. It may come from full blown illusions or partial truths like, "I deserve this, This is the last time, I'm doing this for your good, I should, This hurts me more than it hurts you." How charitable!

Think of an illusion you lived under for many years. How did you see through it finally? You will derive great benefit once you can see through yet another illusion. What a unique gift it is to trace the fallacies in one's approach to life or in one's thinking about life, religious or secular!

The purpose of this review according to Ignatius is that once such an experience has been understood and carefully observed, the person is wary the next time there is static or a distraction of this sort.

335. LISTENING TO THE SPIRIT

This is a very significant insight of Ignatius for those who are progressing in the spiritual life. He mentions that the action of the good spirit is delicate and gentle and delightful. He compares it to the natural experience of water penetrating a sponge. The idea of a good angel is not that there is another spirit directing us, but rather a sense of being drawn easily to doing what is good. It is like being directed to move in a particular way and yet there is no other tangible force. It sometimes feels like it is coming from within and sometimes the attraction appears to be from the outside. It is basically a connection, a flow. It is not as specific as inside or outside, it is more like the experience of fresh air that on one hand is around you and yet is experienced within. It is the ease of moving with the wind at your back; it is outside yet we become one with the flow.

Ignatius contrasts this good spirit, the ease of being and doing good, with the effort, heaviness and doubts that can also affect one's daily life. These seem to be outside forces that disturb one's inner peace, but the cause could be inner turmoil, like feeling pushed or coaxed to do something. There is a resistance, and a sense of being dissatisfied. Ignatius calls it noisy and disturbing. When we are invited to do something or go somewhere, one day it seems natural, appealing and fitting and on other occasions, scratchy. Maybe the timing is off.

There are certain types of people for whom an entirely different approach may be needed. Some of these personalities might be ones who were raised by addictive, authoritarian, emotionally repressed parents, who indoctrinated their children with rigid beliefs. For someone who was so programmed and negatively influenced, anything that is freeing or creative seems foreign and unrealistic. It will at least seem inappropriate to one's pattern of behavior.

So Ignatius recommends the basic approach to be gentle encouragement as well as a consistent appeal to reason. There may be a tendency to react to the violence the person experienced in life with anger and disappointment, but that would be counterproductive. It is important to be aware of his conditioning and to avoid exhortations so that the person can make his own leap of faith, by his own choice. Listening to his own inspirations as the source of his decision will confirm a new belief in himself. He is indebted to no one. He is free.

336. BEING REASONABLE

A caution is offered to those who are experiencing consolation. Consolation is often described in glowing terms, as peace, satisfaction, wonder and acceptance. When one feels gifted or favored by God there might be the tendency to make a resolution, to do something special with one's life. So Ignatius advises caution in distinguishing a feeling from a state of mind. Resolution is a decision that comes from a clear vantage point and involves action. The commitment assumes that the original position is valid, otherwise it can lose its meaning and value.

As Ignatius has explained in previous annotations, one ought not to make decisions while experiencing desolation. So too in consolation equal care must be taken before approval or execution is given to decisions.

A good example of this is that while giving to the poor is a gospel mandate, a laudable practice, and undoubtedly a great apostolate it has significant limitations. Personal scrutiny is essential to implement this wonderful theorem. The consoling invitation "come follow me" is another example. Yet it can only be lived in and through one's unique response. And so while the consolation can be as strong as the call, the resolution might or might not involve any change in the person's life.

EDITOR'S NOTE 1 In countries where civil rights workers are killed, the poor are brutalized. A poor farm lady fed the soldier boys who crossed her farmland. They were all her people and God's people, all helpless victims of society, pawns of military leaders, fodder of armies. The government soldiers warned her not to feed her own people and then they killed her for feeding them. The soldiers were told that they did a good thing in killing this lady. Their ideals were so distorted that they were convinced that they were justified in murdering her for their country. (Of course, their country was her country. Country is a word for a group of people. The excuse for killing was the word "country.") Killing her was not enough however, they burned her farm and killed her children - "for the country"! Fanaticism, condemnation, obligation and then secrecy worked together to foster evil. # 332

What makes illusions so plausible? Do people believe only what they want to believe? Do they naturally prefer the darkness?

Our society has condemned the drug dealers and barons of the world, but praised the arms dealers and CIA. Our country thrives on weapons sales, other countries flourish on drug sales. Thousands die of drug related disease and crime; millions perish with weapons donated or purchased with taxes from major military powers. How do we become indoctrinated and quietly justify such evil? By not seeing! How often do we act out of obligation, insecurity and fear? As often as we do not see! If the livelihood of our family depended on weapons or drug sales, or if our job title was Director of Central Intelligence Activities for the President of the United States would we resign, or act in secret? There but for the situation they are in, am I.

337. RULES FOR THE DISTRIBUTION OF ALMS

Ignatius directed certain retreatants to pray in detail about the commandments, the capital sins, one's mental faculties and the fives senses # 239 - 248. Ignatius also gave comprehensive steps for retreatants who needed help in making important decisions, Annotations # 169 - 189. This present chapter is for anyone who is concerned about charitable distribution of wealth. Some repetition of the rules for decision making will be noticed since the discernment process is similar when applied to the ministry of distributing alms.

338.

If I distribute alms to relatives, friends or others to whom I am attached, there are four things that must be considered.

First, the desire to give material things should be motivated by the love of God and the service of others. The primary awareness then is that the love I feel is by the grace of God, who is the source of all love.

339.

Second, while planning this decision to distribute wealth, I should make an objective consideration in the following way. I will imagine a person whom I have never known, and whom I wish would make a correct and propitious decision in the distribution of his wealth. I will observe closely the course of action that I would advise him to follow. Can I see the good effects clearly and the apostolic value without a shadow of a doubt?

Can I follow the same advice in my present situation?

340.

Third, I will confirm my decision by using a projective technique to picture myself in other circumstances. If this was my final decision or one that I was asked to make at the hour of my death, what priorities would I consider important.

341.

Fourth, a further projection entails picturing myself after my death, conversing with Jesus. As I look back from that heavenly perspective what elements regarding this distribution seem most appropriate.

342.

When one is favorably inclined toward certain persons to whom he wishes to give alms, let him consider the four previous rules and test the authenticity of his affection by them. Once he is clear of any inordinate attachments, his decision will be free of any doubts or regrets.

343.

For those who are able to distribute wealth at their own discretion or who are appointed to distribute material goods, care must be taken that they do not feel personally possessive of this wealth. To be Christlike in the amount the distributor retains and truly selfless in dispensing these goods, the rules above can provide the necessary discernment.

344.

In basic economic considerations, conscientiousness in income and expenses enables a person to do more with the same resources. Regarding financial matters that concern oneself and one's household, as far as it is possible, it is better to imitate the example of Jesus who was trusting of His disciples and generous to all who called to Him.

345. SOME NOTES CONCERNING SCRUPLES

The meaning of scruple is a small weight, or in pharmaceutical terms, 20 grains. In psychological terms, its common meaning is a doubt or hesitancy that prevents a person from acting decisively. Since retreat time is expected to be one of great light, clarity of perception and confidence in response, any wavering must be treated as an obstacle to prayer.

346.

Ignatius first clarifies that an erroneous judgment is not a scruple. A woman might feel bad about forgetting her friend's anniversary and then find out later she was mistaken. So she was upset about nothing: erroneous judgment but not a scruple. Ignatius gives a good example of a person who steps on some straw that was in the form of a cross and thinks he has sinned. He has not sinned, nor was it a scruple, but simply a wrong judgment.

347.

In the case of the person who stepped on the straw in the form of a cross, if he continues to be anxious about the matter, if he fluctuates between it being a sin or not, this hesitancy and doubt qualifies as a scruple.

348.

Erroneous judgments are problematic and painful and a rather common occurrence. More information is necessary to clarify these mistaken beliefs and people often live in these illusions until out of desperation or courage they seek the truth.

With regard to the second example of the scruple described above, the soul-searching necessary for liberation may be long and arduous. Ignatius speaks of his own bouts with scrupulosity and it was just as difficult as he describes.

349.

If one has a delicate conscience, he will feel tempted to be excessively introspective and in the process will be easily disturbed. And so he will be overly sensitive to his own thoughts, words and deeds and in the process might think himself to be unworthy.

If one has a lax conscience, he will be tempted to have no parameters to his behavior and to consider himself beyond reproach.

350.

And so the solution is "Know thyself". If one has a tendency to be lax and he is aware of it and if he wishes to do something about it he ought to take more care in ordering his life, scheduling his time and fidelity to regular reflection.

If someone knows he has a delicate conscience, moderation and inner peace must be the main criteria rather than perfection.

351.

Ignatius wanted individuals in spite of errors, fears, scruples and the powerful influences of authority to above all listen carefully to their own inspirations. There is a precious and graced center within each person. It gives the truest direction to finding the pearl of great price, that one and only future that no one else is privy to, yours.

To fulfill one's vocation in life, whether it is to be the founder of a new religious community, to travel to Jerusalem or Tibet, to give one's life for the service of refugees or to be a parent creating a human life, how will you know? How can one be certain?

Trust yourself; discover good ends and good means; and take courage, for while the seas may be rough, the presence of God will be your guide.

352. RULES FOR THINKING WITH THE CHURCH

While the retreat is basically an individual experience, there is need to make some reference to the person in his relationship with the community of the Church. After describing in detail the power of the scripture and the value of a life of prayer Ignatius gives a vote of approval for what was later called the precepts of the Church.

353.

Ignatius speaks of the gift of being open to new truths, a readiness to hear truth from new directions. He asks that the retreatant listen for and think about a good interpretation on the statements of another. When error is clearly the case, and we must correct the speaker, all kindness is recommended. He applies this presupposition from Annotation # 22 to the Church.

354.
Participation in the sacraments on a regular basis will be of mutual benefit to the person and the community. The resource of the sacrament of reconciliation is a constant reminder of our inseparable relationship with God through Jesus. In particular, the Eucharist, our profession of faith and our unity with Jesus at this covenant meal gives us strength for our journey.

355.
Belonging to a community of the followers of Jesus, provides us with frequent opportunities to be with people at prayer, in times of initiation, mourning and celebration. These ritual times of prayer complement our own daily and personal prayer periods.

356.
We can not admire too much those who have given their lives for the welfare of others. No greater love is there. For those who have been on the front lines of the justice movement, for the peacemakers, for those who take care of the sick, how could we list even the categories of those who have imitated Christ in their corporal and spiritual works of mercy! Each of these dedicated souls is truly the Church that Jesus desired to institute and see spread to the far corners of the earth.

357.
People who dedicate their lives to the disadvantaged and the world's neediest are true believers in the Resurrection as they lay down their life for His sheep. In a dramatic sense these people are choosing poverty rather than the riches of the world. It is obedience to His will and a pure imitation of His labor. These are the authentic vows of a Christlike life.

358.
The saints who have gone before us were ordinary people who lived extraordinary lives. To remember their sacrifices, to venerate their goodness and to tell their story give a broader perspective to the history of our salvation and remind us of the various works of the Spirit.

359.

To commemorate together the feasts of the year appointed by the Church joins us in unity whether the days be fasting or celebrating. To make sacrifices with others in almsgiving, service or other vigils simply works miracles in the community. When two more are gathered Jesus promised to be there.

360.

Churches and other buildings are structures not just of stone and mortar, but were formed by the will, work and sacrifices of thousands of generous people. To see what they represent, the spirit which inspired them and the people they served is worthy of our admiration, gratitude and veneration.

361.

As with the commandments of old, relevant mandates for living in peace with God and neighbor, so too the Church has precepts which foster and enhance a deeper relationship with the Eucharistic community.

362.

We should be more ready to approve and praise the behavior of others than to find fault with them. When their actions are not praiseworthy, rather than speak ill of them to others, it may be profitable to discuss their bad conduct with those who can apply a remedy.

363.

When you read theology, see the context in which it was composed, the good intentions as well as the limited insights. When Jesus preached to His disciples at the Last Supper, he consoled and encouraged them repeatedly, JOHN 14 - 17. Positive Doctors of the Church inspired people to love and serve God in all things with great affection and optimism. The scholastic type of theologian was more defensive, somewhat threatened and even critical, taking as his purpose to refute on one hand and justify on the other.

364.

It would be difficult to make a fair comparison between the saints of the past and our modern, even still living saints. Each is a child of God, all are fully human, each is inspired with the same Spirit and all their good works flowed from the grace of Christ.

365.

Can you think the opposite? Can you debate one side of an issue strongly and be equally convincing from the contradictory point of view?

Can you recall a time when you thoroughly believed something; and then, you experienced something or you learned some new information and your view changed completely? You actually thought the opposite!

Earlier, Ignatius wrote in detail regarding the quality of "indifference," Annotation # 23. An example would be that while a person might find poverty despicable in itself, he might choose it if it meant he could serve with Christ who is poor.

366.

We are all God's creations, by God's design, by God's grace. While we speak of Jesus as Savior, that He came to save the world and all the world is saved through Jesus, we must be careful and sensitive as we speak these mysteries and discuss them with others. First, because they are mysterious beliefs. Second, everyone does not think and believe the same, yet all are loved by God equally. Third, differences among nations and religions and language are so great that all do not even have the same name for the creator.

How often have you witnessed the antagonistic yet overtly pious inquisition, "Are you saved?" Irrelevant, unproductive, even hostile discussions can arise about God, love and salvation.

367.

Ignatius wisely wrote, "We should not make it a habit of speaking much of predestination." It was a theory based on the notion of dualism. When one sees sunlight, it can be traced to its source, the sun. When one sees darkness, it can not be traced to a radiant black ball in the sky. Darkness is the limitation of light, the absence of light. Darkness has no essence. Even a candle can dispel the darkness. There is no such "thing" as darkness. So too with all humanity, we are all images of God the least no less than the greatest.

368.

Faith is the daily living of a powerful grace. It is shown in personal compassion, service to people and in reverence for life. Faith is not a five letter word. It is one of the three things that last. It is a lifetime. It is a gift. We live it like life one decision, one action, one person, one day at a time.

369.

Grace inspires us to do good works out of love. Grace and faith are ways of speaking about the mystery of God's love and presence. We must not speak of grace as though it conflicts with our free will, nor of faith as though it were superior to service. There is a mysterious connection between these virtues as Jesus giving an example by washing the feet of His disciples.

370.

Persons who have been raised under a dictatorship at home, in religion or under a repressive government may have little or no understanding of freedom. For them the only thing they have known is intimidation and repression. Fear and punishment represent the Standard of the world, not Christ's Standard.

Fear was never the style of Jesus, nor the style of the Spirit. You are my Beloved Son, My favor rests on you, Be not afraid, Abba Father! This is the God that Jesus revealed to us. This is the way to the Father.